Youth Ministry
and
Parents

This book is just what we need in Catholic youth ministry to put our values and beliefs about family into practice in our parish communities. The stories, humor, and examples in this book make me feel at ease in trying new ways to reach families. The research and resources give me the tools I need to really make the connection. I can't wait to tell people about this practical and enjoyable resource that will improve our ministry with youth and their families.

—Tom East, director for the Center for Ministry Development

Filled with wisdom, real-life stories and practical tips, this book is a must-read for every youth minister. It's also an easy read, due to Leif Kehrwald's conversational style and natural inclination toward encouragement and support. If you are new in ministry, this book will be a career saver. If you're a veteran, you'll be thrilled to have all these insights, references, and bits of information in one place.

Reading this book was like having a conversation with a good friend. I found myself nodding my head in agreement, highlighting quotations, and bookmarking favorite pages. I kept wanting to read just one more chapter, until I finished the book! Leif has made a wonderful contribution to the fields of youth ministry and family ministry.

—Lisa-Marie Calderone-Stewart, EdD, associate director of the Milwaukee Archdiocese Office for Schools, Child, and Youth Ministries and author of eighteen books with Saint Mary's Press

Youth Ministry and Parents

Secrets for a Successful Partnership

Leif Kehrwald

Saint Mary's Press
Winona, Minnesota

Genuine recycled paper with 10% post-consumer waste. Printed with soy-based ink. 50620

The publishing team included Laurie Delgatto and Barbara Murray, consulting editors; Mary Koehler, permissions editor; Brooke E. Saron, copy editor and production editor; Lynn Riska, typesetter; Kimberly K. Sonnek, designer; cover images by Rubber Ball Productions; manufacturing coordinated by the production services department of Saint Mary's Press.

Printed in the United States of America

Printing: 9 8 7 6 5 4 3 2 1

Year: 2012 11 10 09 08 07 06 05 04

ISBN 088489-789-3

Library of Congress Cataloging-in-Publication Data

Kehrwald, Leif, 1957
    Youth ministry and parents : secrets for a successful partnership / Leif Kehrwald.
    p. cm.
ISBN 0-88489-789-3 (pbk.)
    1. Church work with youth—Catholic Church. 2. Parent and teenager—Religious aspects—Catholic Church.   I. Title.
BX2347.8.Y7 K44 2004
259'.23—dc21

                          2003014169

To the Catholic community of Saint Patrick's, Spokane, Washington.

To the parents of teens at Saint Pat's, who had enough parenting left over to finish raising me.

To all those who remember the Youth House, especially those who lived there, worked there, and shared their lives with teens in Hillyard.

Author's Acknowledgments

No book is a solo effort.

I am forever grateful to my editorial colleagues and mentors at Saint Mary's Press for encouraging me to write this book and for offering ideas, suggestions, critique, and affirmation along the way.

A great portion of the "practical" value of this book comes as a result of my interviews with folks on the front lines of youth ministry. I am grateful to the following people for their candid and expert words of insight: Craig Allan, Ann LaBeck, B. J. Levad, Donna McIntosh, Maryelyn Scholz, and Cathy Walz.

A brainstorm hit me one day last winter: "This book needs a foreword." So I e-mailed my friend and colleague Michael Theisen, in Rochester, New York, to ask whether he would write it. He responded by saying he had never written a foreword but would give it a shot. I believe it is the best foreword I have ever read, and it just may be the best part of this book. **Don't skip the foreword!** Thank you, Michael.

Contents

Foreword

by Michael Theisen

One of the first truths acknowledged by those of us involved in faith formation is that learning is a lifelong experience. And the longer our own ministerial life gets, the more *experience* seems to play a part in our own understanding of ministry. I began in youth ministry as a newly married twenty-something in Richmond, Virginia, in the 1980s, when youth ministry was just beginning to find its own identity within the Catholic Church. In those early years, I often found myself wondering why so many of the teens' parents failed to "get it" when raising their adolescents. The teens I ministered to and with would often complain about the parental injustices they had to endure, or they would share how misunderstood they felt by their parents. I listened and, being closer to their age than their parents' age, understood very clearly what the problem was.

Inevitably I grew older and, in the process, gained more experience as both a parent and a youth minister. Soon I approached that magical line that brought me closer to the age of the parents of the teens rather than to the age of the teens themselves. I could see my solid understanding of the problems between parent and teen graying, along with my hair. I began to see more clearly from the perspective of the parent generation and discovered a new reality in my ministry: parents just don't get a fair shake from many youth ministers or youth ministry programs. Many parish programs tend to largely ignore parents, or at best put up with parents while sponsoring wonderful and exciting programs for the youth. The efforts, often engaging for the young people, actually contribute to the divide in understanding between parent and teen.

It was no mistake that my epiphany occurred simultaneously with my own children's rise into the world of adolescence. After two master's degrees (in social work and in religious education, no less), I thought I had the parenting of teens all figured out. I thought it was as easy as all the parent education talks I had given over the years. But life, like parenting, is puzzling at times, and it certainly does not always follow the patterns and suggestions found in college textbooks. I experienced firsthand my own teens' "rebellion" from parental authority, their cries of "unfair" at our rules, and I was forced to combat their moans and groans about going to church and to religious education classes. How could they? These were *my* children, and I *knew* what teenagers were like; after all, they were *my* job, *my* ministry.

Through the reality-based education in life that I endured, I learned that I don't have all the answers to the questions of life and faith. And neither does any parent, teen, or youth minister, for that matter. I also realized that we all—parents, teens, and youth ministers—can find a greater and more comforting wisdom when, together, we share our experiences, including our failures and frustrations, and work together toward the next step instead of reaching for the elusive fulfillment of the final answer.

The necessity for making this parental journey together was wonderfully illustrated for me during a parish-based program on communication that I sponsored for all the ninth graders and their parents. Ninth grade is one of the key transitional years for parents and teens (as are the first year of junior high and the last year of high school), and getting the two generations together to talk, and more importantly to listen to one another, is usually a gift in and of itself for all involved.

During this particular program, the teens were reporting some of the areas they wanted their parents to re-examine in light of the teens' growing maturity and independence. One girl had been rather vocal throughout the program about how "unfair" her mother was with rules, especially regarding curfew and dating. When it came time for the teens to share their list of issues along with their specific concerns, the girl could not wait to tell the group of about 200 how restrictive her mother was with allowing her to date. She complained that all her friends were able to go out on dates by themselves and did not have to come home until midnight; she wanted her mom to fall into line with the "rest of the world."

I glanced over at the girl's mom sinking down in her seat. I knew she was a single mother who was struggling to keep up with the lives and needs of her three children. She, like so many parents these days, lacked the support of another parent to help her during those difficult hours of parenting and decision making that often occur after a full day at work and before the dinner table has been cleared and the dishes washed. The mother seemed defeated by her outgoing and adventurous daughter. Her aloneness and helplessness at that moment were easy to sense.

I brought the daughter's concern to the gathered community, because she had already made it fairly public by that time. I asked her whether she would like to see who else in this room was allowed to go out alone on dates. Of course the girl, confident in her stance, couldn't wait for the poll. I asked for a show of hands from all her peers who were living by her desired standard of dating. All hands remained down. In that moment the fallacy of "the rest of the world" was revealed, and the mother discovered, perhaps for the first time in a long time, that she was *not* alone. This communal affirmation had an immediate impact upon the mother. She perked back up in the pew. Renewed by the fact that she wasn't way off base, that she wasn't the only one, as her daughter had convinced her to believe, she discovered that she was indeed on the right parenting path.

It became very clear to me at that moment that effective ministry has more to do with supporting the communal journey of the family than with solving problems, planning programs, or seeking what might bring the biggest turnout. We need to walk this journey together as parish ministers, parents, and teens because the road is long, with many twists, turns, and divides that force families to choose among competing directions, usually without the proper signage to guide them. Who wants to make that trip alone? Who can? Yet many of us parents and church ministers have tried. And though some early success may be reported, the final tally is usually less than desirable. It is time for those of us in the church to embark on an intentional and direct partnering with parents to effectively minister to our young people.

We *know* that it takes a village to raise a child, and we *know* that it takes a whole church to effectively minister to our youth, but we have yet to fully incarnate those ideals as a church. Youth ministers are likely to say, "I'm here for the youth" or "When I get the time, I'll hold a parent program." We start in the wrong place and then end up wondering why parents aren't helping out more or why they aren't making the youth-group activities a higher priority in their family's life. The fact is that we, the youth ministers, are the ones who took the wrong turn early in our efforts and in selecting our own paradigms by thinking that it was *our* job to form teens in faith.

When I was a social-work student in graduate school, I found myself having to write the word *family* quite often, so I developed a shorthand symbol for the word that involved writing a capital *F* and circling it, which helped me keep up with my note-taking. Several years later, after getting into parish ministry, I discovered I was writing the word *faith* a lot. At first I resorted to the Ⓕ technique that had served me so well, until one day I went home to look over my notes and came across the following sentences:

"Every teen's Ⓕ is dependent upon his Ⓕ."

"The Ⓕ of a teen impacts his Ⓕ."

What statement did I mean to write? Which came first—faith or family? In examining the statements both ways, each had a significant truth to it. I immediately began to see the problem with my shorthand as well as with my paradigm of ministry to young people. It was indeed a moment of (F). I had been going about my ministry to youth as if I were responsible for their faith formation. I had placed the parents in the grandstands—as somewhat involved but ultimately as passive fans cheering on the work of our youth ministry team. It took some adjustments and some increased teamwork, but I gradually discovered the truth that was there all along: *You cannot have* (F) *without* (F). Should it be any other way?

I often find myself saying, "If only I knew then what I know now, I would have done such a better job with . . ." I'm sure you can complete the sentence yourself. Who among us would not want to have the insight and experience gleaned from the accumulation of all the mistakes and missteps made over the years? We would all be more effective at parenting, at ministering, and at faith formation. What we've needed to move us out of the rut of "my ministry" and toward the embrace of lifelong faith formation is a guide, someone with both the experience and the words to bring parents and youth ministers together in an effective ministerial alliance. As you turn the pages, my guess is you'll discover what I did—that a guide has arrived.

I hope you feel as affirmed and challenged as I did upon discovering the wisdom that Leif offers all of us in the church village. His insights, gleaned from years of trial and error as a youth and family minister, as a parent, and as a diocesan director, provide the reader with a necessary resource for moving toward shared responsibility for the lifelong faith formation of the entire family system.

It's not uncommon for people to mistakenly refer to the *foreword* of a book as a *forward*. A *foreword* is an introduction to a book, while *forward* means, among other things, "to advance to the front or toward the future, to move ahead." I believe both definitions are at work here. With Leif's stories and insights serving as both model and motivation, it's obvious that the only way to move forward in our ministry with young people is by partnering with parents, which in the end is good news for the whole Church.

Forward, indeed!

Introduction

Back in the Good Ol' Days

I became a youth minister while I was still a youth. In my second year at Gonzaga University, in Spokane, Washington, a local pastor convinced me and three of my buddies to establish a youth group at a suburban church. In his mind we had all the necessary traits: boundless energy, willingness to do nutty things, some musical talent, a love for kids (heck, we were still there ourselves), and an emerging, maturing faith. Apparently we had the right combination of ingredients, for within a few short months, we had teens coming out of the woodwork for the "youth Mass" and weekly youth group meeting.

In the eyes of those kids, the four of us could do no wrong. Their adoring smiles stroked my ego like nothing has since. It was a heady experience for us. We invited the kids to sing, and they sang; we asked them to engage in a crazy icebreaker, and they did it with gusto; we asked them to consider opening their hearts to a relationship with Jesus, and many of them did that as well. God seemed so alive in those kids and in me. I was surely called to youth ministry.

By the time I reached my last year in college, I was working nearly full time for another church in Spokane and living in a parish-owned house dubbed the Youth House. Kids would drop in at all hours, day or night, just to hang out, watch television, play Ping-Pong, or perhaps seek some guidance. From the Youth House we ran the youth ministry and faith formation programs for junior and senior high kids. I was newly married, and my wife, Rene, and I lived and worked side by side while we finished our degrees. The year was 1979.

Though I found it easy to connect with kids, those creatures called their parents confused and intimidated me. I repeatedly fumbled and stumbled when encountering them. One parent cornered me after a Sunday worship, demanding to know why her son wasn't able to recite the Lord's Prayer. "When are you going to teach the traditional basic prayers to all these teens?" My throat dried up, my mind went blank, and not a single word escaped my lips. All I could do was nod my head. I know now that I was more interested in being popular with the kids (my perceived job security) than I was in teaching them things I didn't think would interest them.

On another day Don, a youth group regular and a junior in high school at the time, popped his head in the door of the Youth House and said, "If my mom calls, tell her I just left here and I'm walking home." Sure enough, an hour later Don's mom called for him. I said, "He just left to walk home." Turns out Don had told his mom he was going to the Youth House to hang out (good thing), but instead he went to the arcade to blow his allowance (bad thing), and he got me to cover for him (stupid thing). Like I said, in those days I was still pretty much a youth myself.

One more story: A girl in the youth group—I'll call her Jennifer—appeared to be hit extra hard by adolescence. She didn't seem happy, wasn't popular, was always seeking attention, and was generally out of sorts most of the time. In my idealism and ministry fervor, I decided Jennifer simply needed Jesus living in her heart. Who better to facilitate that than me? So, amidst all my other responsibilities and relationships, I made Jennifer my personal ministry project. At first I thought I could have her squared away with Jesus by May of her sophomore year, but she proved to be a tougher nut to crack.

I did not give up. Throughout Jennifer's high school years, I made it a point to reach out to her by including her in activities and conversations with others, attending her cross-country races, and offering spiritual counseling to her when appropriate. Jennifer and I became pretty good friends, and though I was employing all the right ministry tactics—meeting her on her turf, and so on—I always felt like something deeper was going on with Jennifer that she wasn't sharing with me.

Several years after Jennifer graduated from high school, and after Rene and I had moved out of the Youth House and into other ministries, we received a wedding invitation from another girl who had been in the youth group with Jennifer. Her wedding served as a reunion for many of the old youth group gang.

At the reception I found Jennifer and struck up a conversation. I asked her all the usual things: How's college? Do you have a job? Do you have a boyfriend? Then I asked, "How are your folks?" With a sad look in her eyes, she told me that her parents had split right after she graduated. Their separation and divorce were sort of a relief to her because the two of them fought loud and long throughout her high school years. All this was news to me.

For three years I had made a special effort to reach out to Jennifer, to attend to her spiritual needs, to be a friend and adult role model, to connect with her in the places important to her—school, sports, band, and so on. But it hadn't even occurred to me to connect with Jennifer in the key arena of her home life. It never crossed my mind to explore her relationship with and feelings about her parents. It never struck me as strange that she never talked about her folks.

By the time of the wedding reception, it was too late, of course, for me to be of much help to Jennifer. Quite frankly she didn't need help anymore. She had worked through the issues and moved on. All those years when I thought I was helping her, Jennifer was merely tolerating me.

Parents Make a Difference

While I was doing youth ministry in the late '70s and early '80s, kids complained about their parents just as they do today. Back then I sided with the kids and tried to strategize how to advocate against their parents. Memories of my having similar complaints about my parents were still fresh and clear. Parents were obstacles to maneuver around in order to have the kind of youth program I envisioned. *Get Out of My Life, but First Could You Drive Me and Cheryl to the Mall? A Parent's Guide to the New Teenager* (Farrar, Straus, and Giroux, 2002), by Anthony E. Wolf, is a book for parents of young teenagers. This title fits the attitude we youthful youth ministers had toward parents in the Youth House days. Drive, bake cookies, and write checks when we need money, but otherwise get lost. We know teenagers better than you do.

It never occurred to me that parents could be our partners in fulfilling our vision of evangelization and faith formation for those kids. It's no secret that parents are crucial to the faith formation of their children and teens; therefore I contend that parents are crucial to effective youth ministry efforts. Put quite simply a working partnership with parents will yield a substantially more vibrant and effective youth ministry program.

"Youth Ministry: Attitudes and Opinions" (Winona, MN: CMMS, 2000), a recent study commissioned by Saint Mary's Press, shows that you, the youth ministry leader of today, likely understand this need for partnership far better than I did twenty-some years ago. First, you are probably older than I was then. About 84 percent of youth ministers we surveyed in the study are over thirty, and 56 percent are over forty. This means you are likely a parent yourself. Second, of the youth ministers we surveyed, the top-ranked need for youth ministry resources was on the topic of parents' understanding and being involved in adolescent faith development. The fifth-ranked need for resources was on the topic of exploring family-based youth ministry. The field of youth ministry has evolved into a more collaborative process involving parents, families, and other ministry and community efforts that impact the lives of teens.

About This Book

Some of the questions I failed to ask in my youth ministry days might be in the forefront of your mind:

- How can I connect with parents of teens?

- How do I get more parents involved in our youth ministry program?

- How do I get more involved in the lives of parents and families?

- How do parents impact the faith growth of teens today?

- How do I effectively and *practically* partner with parents to nurture the faith growth of teens?

- How do I assist parents in their role as the primary faith influence in the lives of teens?

- How do I find time to work with parents when I have so many other responsibilities?

If those questions are on your mind, this book is for you. In the chapters that follow, I explore what a working partnership between youth minister and parents looks like. In my recounting of interviews with other youth ministers, I highlight what congregations are doing well in their efforts to connect with parents, and I offer suggestions for replicating those strategies.

I explore the various relational issues, concerns, and myths between parents and teens. From a human development viewpoint, I look at the tasks related to adolescence (teens) and midlife (parents). Those tasks are amazingly similar, making for an interesting, and sometimes tumultuous, adolescent family life. It is vitally important to anchor your understanding of adolescent development in the context of family life-cycle growth. For good or ill, the family nearly always has the most influence on the formation and growth of teenagers.

I also explore how the family impacts the conversion, spirituality, and faith of the teenager—and vice versa. Parents and families tend to resist change—even positive change—because it upsets the balance of roles and relationships. When a young person discovers God's gracious activity in his or her life, responds to it, and begins to grow into a personal relationship with Jesus Christ, we celebrate this young person's conversion. But all too often, his or her family, at best, has no idea how to handle this change and, at worst, makes efforts to change the young person back to the way he or she was. If your youth ministry efforts are working, then young people are responding to God's gracious activity in their lives. If you expect those changes to be lasting, you need to help families embrace the spiritual growth you encourage. I explore several specific strategies for doing just that.

Last, I explore what I call the mutuality of involvement. It's only one side of the coin when you ask how you can get parents more involved in your youth ministry program. You must also ask how you can be more involved in the lives of parents and families. You must win the right to be heard. Before parents will embrace your agenda, they must know that you understand their agenda. In the same way that effective youth ministry must meet kids on their turf, you must let parents know that you understand the struggles and concerns they have. You must also recognize that parents know their teenage sons and daughters better than anyone, and you can do this by creating an atmosphere for them to share their knowledge and concerns about their kids and by responding with sincerity.   .

Each chapter concludes with nuts-and-bolts suggestions for youth ministry programming. You will be able to apply these ideas as you learn them.

As a youth minister, you opened this book and read these pages, perhaps seeking answers to a certain set of problems and challenges in your ministry. The goal of this book is not to solve those problems. Rather my goal is to give you a new and better set of challenges in your ministry. I am confident that as you read these pages you will see the paramount importance of partnering with parents in your ministry with teens. I am also confident that as you incorporate some of the suggestions scattered throughout this book at least some of your original problems and challenges will fade into new and exciting invitations for bringing about the Kingdom of God.

Chapter 1

Partnership with Parents

Sphere of Influence

Would you prefer to perform your youth ministry duties from a position of strength or weakness? Strength, of course. That means understanding and working from your own unique sphere of influence. *Sphere of influence* refers to the arena in which you conduct your ministry, exercising some control and having (at least some) influence on the outcome. Your sphere of influence is the place where you take heat for mistakes and get credit for successes. When you work from within your sphere of influence—rather than trying to change things that are out of your control—you experience more success, and your sphere tends to expand, allowing you greater influence.

If you succeed in reaching a small, core group of kids, you will likely see your ministry expand as those kids reach out and invite others. You might also find parents and other adults in the community listening to you more intently, for "Look how the youth program has grown!" Suddenly your sphere of influence is reaching beyond your primary responsibility.

Take a moment to complete the simple exercise on the following pages.

Naming and Reflecting on Your Sphere of Influence

How would you name your primary sphere of influence in your ministry setting? Perhaps your job title names it well; perhaps other descriptors are needed. Name the "place" where you have power to influence what is done and how things are done. You may not be the one in charge, but perhaps you are a contributing team member. Write down your sphere of influence.

Now, take a moment to reflect on your sphere of influence with respect to parents and family life. Jot down a few positives and negatives. When parents and family is the key lens, what goes well? What is lacking?

Reflect on and jot down your feelings and attitudes toward parents. Be completely honest with yourself.

Bookmark this page so you can refer to it as you read this book. Whenever you get an idea to try something new in your ministry, or to change an existing practice, refer to your sphere of influence. Try to incorporate the change *within* your sphere.

When I conduct workshops for catechetical leaders, I often hear remarks like these:

"If only my pastor could hear this, then we could really move on some new ideas."

"If only my whole team had come with me, we could sit down and make these changes right away."

"As soon as I get home, I'm going to convince the parish council that they have to do things differently."

These statements may indicate a desire to change things outside your sphere of influence, and that change may be hard to come by. What difference, however small, can *you* make? Start there. If it's the right move, others will take note and want to learn from you.

Partnership Implies Relationship

The youth ministry and catechetical staff of Saint Cecilia's in Ashland, Massachusetts, understands the value of partnership. The parish, located about twenty miles outside Boston, is relatively small, and parents are a key component to its effective ministry with young people. The staff succeeds in getting parents involved by being involved with parents.

Donna McIntosh coordinates Saint Cecilia's junior high ministry program and describes some of her efforts to support parents:

We offer several sessions during the year, offering speakers on subjects of genuine interest to parents and families: sexuality awareness, parent-teen communication, AIDS, right to life, and so on. Turnout is really strong. We know each parent, and they know us. They seem confident that we are not going to waste their time.

When parents are supported, and when they have confidence in the parish program, getting them involved is much easier. McIntosh reports:

> We have a wonderful group of parents on our youth board, as well as peer ministers, who help us with different activities. Our parents help us with retreat days and also help when food is needed for activities we're doing. We ask parents to help out with various service projects. We've had the most success when the parents and students work together on a project or activity. For example, we've done activities on friendship and how kids pick their friends, and we involved parents in discussions with their kids. We mixed parents and students so they all have the opportunity to relate to each other.

McIntosh believes these activities enhance rapport between teens and their parents, giving them experiences to talk about and perhaps bridging some of the natural separation that happens during adolescence.

In addition, the Saint Cecilia catechetical team of McIntosh, Janet Wilkinson, and Colleen Wells works closely together. All three ministers have been involved in the parish for years—as parents themselves, as volunteers, and now as staff. "We do everything together," reports McIntosh. "Everyone knows that we're a team." The team members recognize that partnering with parents involves close collaboration with one another.

No need to belabor the obvious: Partnership implies relationship. Parents enter into a relationship with your parish and your youth ministry program when they enroll or simply send their teenagers to the program. Although a lot is implied in that relationship, not much is said about it, leading to unrealistic expectations.

Another obvious point: Just because parents have a relationship with your program, that does not mean they have a relationship with *you*. The *institutional* relationship between the family and the parish is one important factor, but the *personal* relationship between the actual parents and families of kids in your program and you is another, equally important factor. Ideally the institutional relationship and the personal relationship are congruous and reinforce each other.

Though I cannot comment on your personal relationship with parents and families, I can offer helpful insights and a vision for what that institutional relationship ought to look like. Down through the ages, the Church has articulated a vision for the partnership between the church of the parish and the church of the home.

At this point, dear reader, I strongly encourage you to read appendix A, which includes an essay on the vision of the church of the home. In that essay, you will read how the term *domestic church* was not coined in the documents of the Second Vatican Council but rather was resurrected from the early Church fathers. You will read about John Paul II's vision for the family to "become what you are" as a church of the home and his challenge to Church leaders that "no plan for organized pastoral work, at any level, must ever fail to take into consideration the pastoral care of the family" *(Role of the Christian Family in the Modern World [Familiaris Consortio]).* And you will read about the U.S. Catholic bishops' pastoral message to families, *Follow the Way of Love,* in which the bishops proclaim, "As Christian families, you not only belong to the Church, but your daily life is a true expression of the Church" (United States Conference of Catholic Bishops). Imagine what your parish and diocesan ministry programs would look like if you took that statement seriously!

Also in appendix A you will read about a particular spirituality that is conducive to families' finding God's gracious presence in the creases and folds of their daily lives. Indeed the Christian family is holy and sacred, and this fact carries far-reaching implications for all believers, particularly for those who minister to and with youth, their parents, and their families.

Furthermore, as the family is described in ecclesial terms, you would also do well to think of the Church, particularly at the parish level, in *familial* terms. Try this simple exercise: Bring to mind your favorite sayings about home, and simply replace *home* with *church.* Here is what some sayings might sound like:

"There's no place like [church]."
(John Howard Payne, "Home, Sweet Home")

"[Church] is where the heart is."
(Angela Carter, "My Father's House")

"[Church] is the place where, when you have to go there,
They have to take you in."
(Robert Frost, "The Death of the Hired Man")

My personal favorite: "It's always a good day to travel when I'm heading . . . to [church]."

If these sayings sound strange to your ear, that is understandable. You are probably not used to thinking of church in these ways. But why shouldn't you? If you seek to partner with parents and families in your faith formation efforts with youth, you will do well to become more familial in your programs and initiatives.

For the sake of this chapter's conversation on partnership, and as a foundation for reading the remainder of this book, please take a few moments to read appendix A.

Partnership Is Crucial for Effective Youth Ministry

Marge Brewer was the sixth-grade catechist at Saint Patrick's when Rene and I moved into the Youth House. She had been the catechist for this grade for at least the previous twenty-five years. She struck me as a dour, elderly woman with an antiquated approach to faith formation, which she called *CCD,* a new term to her. In my youthful zeal to create a vibrant junior high ministry, I suggested to our pastor that perhaps Mrs. Brewer would like to retire and we could incorporate the sixth graders into the new junior high group. He responded: "Not on your life! Marge has taught most of the parents in this parish, and they *love* her. She's one of our best assets. I know the kids are not too sure about her right now, but you watch. By Christmas they will have grown very fond of her." Sure enough, the pastor was right.

It is futile to think you can do lasting ministry with kids without connecting with their parents. Sure, you can have fun with them, build community for them with other youth, teach them a few things about the Christian tradition, and even introduce them to a personal relationship with Christ. You can model Christian living for them, challenge them to Christian service, and counsel them through some of their struggles. You can become a key faith influence in their lives.

But I'm here to tell you that if you cannot connect with and partner with the young people's parents, much—if not all—of your relational ministry efforts will be short-lived.

One reason for this is that families naturally resist change—even positive change. When your youth program assists kids in their discovery of God's gracious activity in their lives and invites them to respond to it, the kids grow and change, in a positive way. I know it's hard to imagine, but parents and families tend to resist that change. Why? Because it upsets family balance. When you partner with parents for effective faith formation, you can help them embrace and adjust to these changes. I talk more about this in chapter 7.

You must also be realistic. When it comes to faith discovery, the parish youth program is likely *not* the primary sphere of influence for the young person. Research indicates that parents, family, and home life occupy that spot. It only makes sense, then, for you to connect with and partner with parents and families. They can help you accomplish your goals! I talk more about this dynamic in chapter 8.

Remember, this is a partnership. Parents contribute to the lasting faith of youth through initial faith formation, modeling a Christian lifestyle, and providing a home life that is conducive to faith discovery. The parish, the youth ministry program, and you contribute the larger faith community; effective relational ministry; clear, accurate, and developmentally appropriate catechesis; and a further example of healthy Christian living.

Both entities—the parents and the parish—can have powerful evangelical and catechetical influence on young people. But when the two work together in partnership, the impact of both is greatly enhanced.

Recall the example of Saint Cecilia's earlier this chapter. Note that the staff see that getting parents involved means getting involved with parents. The staff know each and every parent. The staff utilize the same relational ministry skills with parents as with kids. They provide program support that meets the real needs of parents. They have won the confidence of parents. I talk more about this idea in chapter 9.

Questions to Ponder

How would you describe the *institutional* relationship between your program and the parents of youth in your program?

How would you describe the *personal* relationship between you and the parents of the youth in your program?

In what ways might your youth ministry program take on a more *familial* nature to enhance your partnership with parents and families?

Chapter 2

Family Stages

For the past several years, at the beginning of a presentation or a workshop with a group of adults, I have been introducing myself and telling the group a bit about my family. In recent years, with teenagers in the house, I have found myself telling the group something like this: "And everything in our house is measured by how much it does or does not 'suck'! Lately it seems pretty much 'everything sucks.' But occasionally something good comes along and I'll hear from one of the boys, 'Gee, Dad, that doesn't suck so bad.'"

We're in the adolescent stage of our family life cycle. Just about everyone can relate to the stage when I introduce my family in that way. And that's my purpose. Some participants identify with that stage because they have teenagers of their own. Others remember the teen years with fondness but don't regret that they have moved on to a new stage. And still others, whose families are younger, feel a little anxious anticipation about the coming teen years.

When one stage of the family life cycle is articulated—even hinted at—the others begin to emerge. Yet the research and study of family stages goes deeper than vague references to typical behaviors during certain predictable periods. If you seek to partner with parents in your youth ministry efforts, you can benefit from a richer understanding of family stages.

Understanding Family Stages

Family life-cycle theory attempts to name the predictable change points that most families encounter as they journey through life together. Though the theory might be helpful for general understanding of family issues and dynamics, not all families experience the "stages" in the same way or even in the same order. If you try to fit each family into a particular mold or category and to draw all your assumptions about that family based on the predetermined characteristics of the mold or category, you are misusing this development theory. In fact, you should use the opposite approach. With the stage categories residing in the background of your mind, you should be able to gain a richer and deeper understanding of the particular concerns and issues of the family, teen, or parent you're encountering at the moment.

At the risk of oversimplifying the concept, you can contemplate the family life-cycle stages in these terms: unattached young adult, married without children, parents with very young children, school-age family, adolescent family, launching family, and family in later life. I reluctantly name the stages in list format because the simple list implies that families move through each stage cleanly, without undue effort, and in proper order. That seldom happens.

Linear Family Life Cycle

One way to "view" the predictable stages of family living over time is in a linear fashion, meaning that family development occurs in the linear dimension of time. Some experts have suggested modifying the term *family life cycle* to *family career,* a term that more accurately captures the linear nature of family life stages and implies the possibility that different families have different career paths, such as divorce, remarriage, cohabitation, and so on (Diana R. Garland, *Family Ministry,* p. 115). Although valid and helpful, this view has limitations.

In an unpublished paper commissioned by Saint Mary's Press in 1999, noted family ministry expert Kathleen Finley describes the linear nature of the family life cycle and defines the different stages:

Although family systems may resist change, the one constant in any family system *is* change, the predictable shifts and stages that a family goes through. In our contemporary Western society, unlike some others, this family life cycle begins with a single young adult. Let's look at how these stages unfold in an intact, middle-class American family and how these stages overlap into other stages.

Single young adulthood. The period of time between a young person leaving the family home and marrying and beginning his or her own family is longer than has been the case in recent generations. During this in-between time, the young adult clarifies his or her values and personality and finishes the process of separating from the family of origin.

The newly married couple. This stage represents the changing of two entire family systems . . . and an overlapping to develop a third subsystem. The new couple has many tasks to achieve together beyond their own intimacy and existence as a separate family unit. They need to work on issues of individual and couple identity, such as time with friends, times of solitude, and developing individual and joint interests. They also need to sort out roles, careers, finances, sexuality, family planning, religion, and spirituality. Many couples describe their first year of marriage as hard or exhausting as well as good, precisely because they have to work out and clarify so many issues.

Early parenthood. The stage of early parenthood brings fresh challenges. The new parents now work to juggle their roles as parents in addition to what they already handle, which—increasingly—is two full-time jobs outside of the home. Part of this stage involves decisions about how to establish a healthy balance as spouses and parents in the midst of many other demands. The couple also need to learn how to relate to their parents as the grandparents of this new generation.

The school-age family. As each child begins to relate to a world beyond the family, to explore friendships and new skills, and to take on more responsibility within the household, the entire family undergoes a shift. One significant challenge during this stage is the building of strong communication and conflict resolution skills—skills that will play a significant role in the next stage.

The adolescent family. The family with adolescents balances the needs and values of the family with the increasing demands and attractions of the adolescents' peer group. The family now needs more flexible boundaries that will allow for both dependence and independence. Each teen establishes his or her own identity and sense of self, while the parents deal with midlife issues and perhaps with aging parents.

The launching family. This family is relatively new because of increased longevity, and it focuses on directing and supporting its young adults in the challenge of building their own independent lives. Not only does this involve a re-grouping of the remaining family members and of the couple, but the process may happen more than once. It is not unusual, for example, for a young adult to attempt independence only to find that he or she needs to return "home" temporarily. At times, this may involve meshing with another family—as in-laws—if there is a marriage. This family also deals with the dying of the older generation.

The aging family. This family deals with retirement and coming to terms with physical limitations. At times, this may include relinquishing power and even becoming dependent on others. Family relationships primarily consist of relationships with adult children and grandchildren—and perhaps great-grandchildren. This family also deals with the death of a spouse as well as that of friends.

Bear in mind that this is a mere outline of predictable stages in a family life cycle, and that each family goes through this cycle in its own unique way. Experiences such as divorce and possible remarriage, a cohabiting couple or a teen pregnancy, for example, make this process much more complex than described here. Other variables, such as ethnicity, economic level, and geographic location, may also be involved. What's more, most families find themselves in more than one stage at a time. School-age families, for example, may have an adolescent, and the adolescent family may be engaged in the challenges of the launching family.

Nonlinear Family Life Cycle

Another way to view the family life cycle is to look at the developmental tasks of families as they relate to natural life passages. Finley relies on the work of William Bridges in *Transitions: Making Sense of Life's Changes* (Reading, MA: Addison-Wesley Publishing, 1980) to define these nonlinear tasks in her paper:

Because change is a constant, whether in families or in individuals, it is helpful for us to understand how change happens in our lives. Although the notion of life passages was popularized by Gail Sheehy in the mid-1970s with her book *Passages,* this concept is anthropological in its origins and has deeply religious roots. Theorists point out that there are three main stages to any life passage: *separation, marginality,* and *reintegration.* (These may be variously named; in William Bridges's excellent book *Transitions: Making Sense of Life's Changes,* he refers to these stages as endings, the neutral zone, and a new beginning.)

In *separation,* something within the individual—or from an external source—impels that person to leave the status quo. When that change comes from outside, for example, the situation may range from graduating from college to losing one's job as a result of "downsizing," to relocating due to health reasons. Examples of the change coming from within might include quitting school, seeking a different job, or moving to a friendlier climate. Either way, that person is leaving the status quo and separating from what is in some way familiar. That involves some discomfort and grieving, even if what the person is leaving behind is not all that pleasant.

Whether from within or without, this change moves the individual to a place of *marginality,* in the midst of stress and uncertainty. What was once comfortable and familiar is now gone, and now the individual struggles to find his or her bearings in a new situation. The individual is no longer in the old setting and yet doesn't really know where to fit in the new and unfamiliar environment. Besides being a time of considerable risk and vulnerability, this is also a time of *tremendous growth,* although it's hard to recognize and identify it as such in the midst of the experience. . . .

With time, however, *reintegration* begins. Life gradually returns to normal as the individual regains a sense of comfort and greater familiarity and begins to emerge into a more stable situation. It is now time to get on with life.

Each of these stages happens over and over again in our lives; they each take time and energy, and each is important to the success of the overall life passage. Although these stages are described here in terms of an individual, they also occur in families. Even when they happen to individuals, they still involve the family of origin to some extent. . . .

A life passage is evident, for example, as a marriage begins, first in the *separation* of a young woman and man from their families of origin and friends, then in the *marginality* of the wedding and honeymoon experience, and finally in the *reintegration* to a new sense of identity as a married couple. Similar stages happen again and again throughout the family life cycle, from the birth of each child to sending each child off to school to the death of a spouse or other family member.

Similar to life passages, another way to image and describe how families grow and develop is through interpersonal processes. In their article "The Epigenesis of Relational Systems," Lyman Wynne and Kenneth Terkelson describe four processes that unfold in families:

1. attachment/caregiving
2. communicating
3. joint problem-solving
4. mutuality

(Adapted; in *Family Process*, vol. 23, pp. 297–318)

In her book *Family Ministry: A Comprehensive Guide*, Diana R. Garland comments on these processes:

"Attachment and caregiving" refers to the bond of affection that develops between family members over time and circumstances. "Communication" refers to sharing interests and exchanging meaning and messages with one another. "Joint problem-solving" refers to sharing and collaborating in tasks, interests and activities. "Mutuality" is the renewing and deepening of the relationship through the previous three processes as the family changes over time.

Each of these processes builds on and assumes those that precede it. Joint problem-solving, for example, must be preceded by attachment. A family will not stick it out through a difficult problem if they are not attached to one another. (P. 123)

What is it that empowers families to successfully navigate from one process to the next? For Kenneth Terkelson, it comes down to *meeting needs*. When families meet the ever-changing needs of its members they "develop a sense of cohesion and create a sense of 'resource sufficiency' that together they have the resources to do what individual members could not do on their own. . . . By contrast, families that fail to meet members' needs typically generate a sense of 'resource scarcity' and family fragmentation" ("Toward a Theory of the Life Cycle").

It must be noted that stress nearly always accompanies change. A family stage shift disrupts rules, roles, and responsibilities. Families feel themselves floundering, searching for new ways to relate to one another and to the world around them. Even change marked by happy events can create stress.

Practical Application for Effective Youth Ministry

So what on earth does all this family development stuff have to do with day-to-day ministry with youth? Good question. You may be tempted to simply assume that because you work with teenagers, all the families of those kids fit nicely into the category of *adolescent families.* But, of course, as soon as you make that assumption, you know it's flawed. A family whose oldest child is a freshman in your program is certainly at a different stage than a family whose third child is a senior in your program. And this is to say nothing of the particular relational needs of families dealing with separation, divorce, single parenting, stepparenting, and so on.

I would offer that the primary purpose for addressing family stages and changes is a strong belief that *moments of change and transition in family life provide opportunities for faith growth.* When families spend time together, build healthy relationships with one another, share meals with one another, solve conflicts and reconcile with one another, they grow not only in well-being but also in faith. If we in the Church help families deal with their change issues, they will be more open to the mission and message we proclaim.

How do we help families navigate the complexities of change? I'd like to suggest two strategies: like-to-like ministry and focus-and-invite ministry.

Like-to-Like Ministry

Earlier I mentioned my youth ministry work at Saint Patrick's Parish in Spokane, Washington. Through the leadership of our pastor (Tom

Caswell) and pastoral associate (Carol Lee), I learned how to do like-to-like ministry. Our approach to ministry at Saint Pat's was relational and personal. We believed (and I still do) that every person in the congregation holds a piece of the truth of God, whom we all seek, and each person deserves to be fully accepted and known. On the pastoral team, we had a couple unspoken rules that applied to the coffee-and-doughnut hour on Sundays: (1) All of us were expected to be there after each service, and (2) we were not to visit with one another; rather, we were to "work the room," visiting with those we knew and those we did not. The point was to connect with people, build relationships, and then, most importantly, look for ways to connect folks with similar needs and similar concerns. This is the essence of relational ministry.

Carol Lee was a master at "working the room." She is one of those people who has a way of putting others at ease. Not long after meeting someone, Carol is learning about their concerns, struggles, heartbreaks, and so forth. But, back in our days at Saint Pat's, Carol knew she could not be as much help to a person as perhaps someone facing a similar struggle. As soon as she could, Carol would introduce people of similar situations, get them started on a visit, and then pull back, allowing them to develop a relationship. She would not betray their confidence, but it didn't usually take long for the people to begin sharing their stories. That is powerful like-to-like ministry.

Focus-and-Invite Ministry

This strategy is similar to like-to-like ministry but is just a bit more systematized. It involves *focusing* on a particular group of parents or families with similar needs, concerns, and circumstances and *inviting* them to come together for mutual support and ongoing learning. For example, if you have a large pool of parents with teenagers, you might choose to focus on those whose oldest child is just entering the adolescent years and invite them to a special session called "Welcoming the Teen Years" or "My Child Has Become a Teenager, Now What?" Or, you might choose parents of high school seniors and call the session "Preparing for the Launch."

The best way to go about doing focus-and-invite ministry is to find out exactly who fits your focus group and then send them a personal invitation. Follow up with general announcements (in the bulletin, from the pulpit, and so on) as reinforcement of the personal invitation and then perhaps a phone call. Let your focus group know that you are trying to understand their issues and concerns and that the session you've planned for them is just that—a special time of support, an opportunity to meet other parents in the same boat, and a time to explore opportunities for ongoing enrichment.

For the focus-and-invite session, you will want to plan carefully to allow for plenty of interaction among participants in large-group, small-group, and one-to-one conversations. You may want to offer some expert input via a speaker or media presentation or from your-self, but don't let that dominate the entire session. Use expert input as a stimulus to get people talking and sharing with one another. You should have a resource table with pertinent books, periodicals, and handouts for participants to browse. You should also have refresh-ments of some sort available. You can conclude the session with a brief discussion about options for ongoing support and enrichment for those who might be interested. Be clear that those options are *optional*.

Through the focus-and-invite strategy, you are communicating to parents that you understand the challenges they face, that you want to help, and that one of the best ways to deal with these challenges is through mutual support and encouragement from others in similar situations.

For both strategies, like-to-like ministry and focus-and-invite ministry, you serve as a catalyst to bring together the folks who are in the best position to help one another.

Questions to Ponder

What are some of the issues and concerns common to all parents of teenagers? In what ways do you address these in your youth ministry program?

In what ways does an understanding of the linear family life-cycle stages help you grasp the developmental tasks of teenage families?

In what ways does an understanding of the interpersonal processes of family development give you insight into the lives of teenage families?

If you were to implement the focus-and-invite strategy, which group of parents would you focus on first? Why?

Chapter 3

Why Parents?

A myth has enough credibility to be believed but not enough to be true. It's a myth that when kids become teens they can't stand their parents. It's a myth that when kids become teens, their parents no longer know how to connect with them. In this chapter I expose these myths for what they are and reveal some truths about parents and teens.

Years ago I was invited to give some workshops for parish leaders in Baton Rouge, Louisiana. I spent the weekend in the home of my colleague and friend who was sponsoring the workshops. He and his wife were parents of four teenagers. My children were elementary school age at the time.

My friend and I were in the house early Saturday evening, and I was fascinated watching the relational dynamics between parents and teens as the teens made and initiated their plans for Saturday night. Each child had his or her own method, but all appeared quite effective.

One son simply walked through the kitchen and out the back door, leaving Mom and Dad to call after him and try to negotiate who, what, where, when, and curfew to his backside. He got away revealing minimal information and gaining maximum latitude.

A daughter remained ensconced in her bedroom until her four friends came to pick her up. They had made intricate and detailed plans for the evening, which involved a questionable movie and other late-night activity that she knew she would never succeed in negotiating on her own. But when her friends filed into the kitchen and she announced their plans to all present, an awkward silence ushered all the girls out the back door.

The other teens used similar tactics to negotiate their Saturday night activities. I was a bit appalled at how the kids seemed to be running the show and manipulating their parents. But the next day, visiting with my friend's wife, she told me that while the chaos of the previous evening was not altogether unusual, long Sunday morning stories from each teen about his or her adventures the previous night were also not unusual. Those stories usually involved comments about poor choices some of the kids' friends had made, while the kids had held back. My friend's wife said to me, "I much prefer the Sunday morning stories over the Saturday night arguments and power plays." Although their style of parenting was not one I could comfortably adopt, my friends had found a way to stay connected with their teens, and the depth of intimacy they shared transcended their activities.

Recently my wife and I were talking about our two late-adolescent sons. In a joking manner, we marveled at the attitudes and behaviors they exhibit at home in contrast to what other adults tell us about our sons. Our friends and the parents of our sons' friends often remark how considerate, mature, helpful, and polite our sons are whenever they see them in church, at school, on the job, and so on. Rene and I looked at each other, and we did not even have to voice the thought shared between us: "Sheesh! Are they talking about the same two boys who live here?"

Our younger son, who is eighteen, is showing all the signs that home is the last place he wants to be, and his parents are the last people he wants to be stuck in the same room with. Consequently any information we get from him arrives as he's running out the door. "I've got to be at work in ten minutes!" "No, I won't be home for dinner." "Yes, I did water the garden." All we get are little snippets of a life so full there doesn't seem to be time to stop, reflect, and talk. An outsider would likely conclude that communication has broken down, that our son doesn't want to have anything to do with his parents, and that we have lost the ability to reach him. Perhaps the myth that teens don't want to communicate with their parents is actually true.

Yet our younger son gives subtle clues that he values his parents and wants to stay connected—a shared glance and rolling of the eyes over something funny on television, a late night chat with his mother about his girlfriend, a lack of argument over attending Mass on Sunday, a word from his friend's parent that he looks up to his old man. No, it's not like when he was ten and worshiped the ground I walked on, but things haven't changed completely. When push comes to shove, when something important is on the line, when he needs genuine comfort and unconditional love, our son seeks out his parents first. There is much happening in his life that is leading him away from home, toward independence and personal responsibility, but he knows he still has his parents to fall back on.

When Push Comes to Shove

When the chips are down, when teenagers feel troubled, they most often turn to their parents first. Family ties are stronger, in most instances, than the tasks of typical developmental growth.

Look at it this way: Every teenager has to figure out how to be an individual and how to find a place in the world. Therefore, every teenager has to figure out "what's me that is not Mom or Dad." This is what the experts call differentiation. This is what some in our society have misnamed teenage rebellion. Every person has to do it. It is not a problem; it is a key task.

It makes sense, then, that parents and teens will experience some friction along the way. You see, parents naturally tend to try to shape their kids in the image and likeness of *themselves,* so when the teens choose to differentiate, parents get a little anxious, which causes tension, which can lead to conflict. Essentially, though, teens are simply doing what they need to do to find their unique spot on the planet. When parents respond with some anxiety and discomfort, they too are simply doing what they need to do. A certain amount of tension and conflict are built into the system—hard to avoid. In fact, if teens and parents sail through the adolescent years with nary a conflict, then I contend that either the teen has not done his or her job of differentiation, the parents have not done their job of maintaining parental responsibility and boundaries, or both have failed.

Through this natural developmental process called maturity, family ties remain stronger than the tensions caused by developmental growth. Picture the parent-teen relationship as a bedrock foundation upon which all this growth takes place. The young person may go days without giving the slightest consideration to that bedrock relationship. So much is happening on other levels, with friends, teachers, peers, self, and so on, that parents do not appear on the radar screen, and neither do chores, family meals, or even picking up after oneself.

But then something may happen—positive or negative—in the life of the teen that takes him or her to a deeper level of meaning and emotion, and suddenly that bedrock, foundational relationship with Mom or Dad becomes paramount, the teen seeks to connect. The parental challenge at this moment is to meet the teenager on his or her level, which probably means setting aside parental frustrations over being ignored for days on end, failed chores, and general lack of participation in the household community. The parent must deal with those issues at another time. At the moment, he or she must be present and available to the teen's needs. This is how to keep the parent-teen relationship in that bedrock, foundational position.

What the Research Shows

The research on parent-teen relationships shows several simple, yet fascinating conclusions:

- Teens want more conversation with their parents.

- Parents want more conversation with their teens.

- Teens wonder why parents don't open up more to them.

- Parents wonder why teens don't open up more to them.

This is a double-edged sword gone dull. Both parents and teens want to communicate with each other, and both wonder why the other isn't more open. In many cases all parents and teens need is a catalyst to help them get started. Doesn't it make sense that your youth ministry program provide that catalyst? Perhaps you can provide the arena for parents and teens to come together on neutral ground. Perhaps you can provide the atmosphere for them to discuss things on a deeper level that they cannot quite get to on their own. Perhaps you can provide the stimulus for them to address troubling or nagging issues they have been avoiding.

I have seen this dynamic occur over and over again between parents and middle-schoolers when I facilitate the "Welcoming the Teen Years" workshop for a local parish or school. Playing catalyst may be one of the most important roles of the youth ministry program.

In their ground-breaking book *Passing On the Faith: A Radical New Model for Youth and Family Ministry,* Merton P. Strommen and Richard A. Hardel address the communication challenges between parents and teens. Referring to a 1960 Search Institute study of Lutheran youth and adults, Strommen and Hardel state, "These youth and parents said they wished they could talk with one another about significant issues, but for some reason this was not a part of their family life" (p. 48).

In 1992 Search Institute conducted another national survey of youth and parents, looking for insight into young people's desire for parent-youth communication. The survey described several typical adolescent issues and then asked: "If you were in the following situations, to whom would you most likely turn for help or advice?"

The choices were:

- a parent or guardian

- a friend my age

- an adult friend (not a relative)

- a priest, minister, or rabbi

- a teacher or school counselor

- nobody

The results:

When having trouble in school, I would turn to . . .

- a parent or guardian = 55 percent

- a friend my age = 15 percent

- a teacher = 17 percent

- all others = 12 percent

When wondering how to handle my feelings, I would turn to . . .

- a parent or guardian = 51 percent

- a friend my age = 21 percent

- nobody = 9 percent

- all others = 18 percent

If some of my friends start using drugs and alcohol, I would turn to . . .

- a parent or guardian = 45 percent

- a friend my age = 19 percent

- a teacher = 10 percent

- an adult friend = 9 percent

- nobody = 9 percent

- a minister or relative = 12 percent

When having questions about sex, I would turn to . . .

- a parent or guardian = 53 percent

- a friend my age = 19 percent

- nobody = 10 percent

- all others = 17 percent

When feeling guilty about something I have done, I would turn to . . .

- a parent or guardian = 40 percent

- a friend my age = 25 percent

- a minister or priest= 11 percent

- nobody = 9 percent

- all others = 15 percent

When deciding what to do with my life, I would turn to . . .

- a parent or guardian = 66 percent

- nobody = 10 percent

- a friend my age = 6 percent

- all others = 18 percent

(Adapted from *Passing On the Faith,* pp. 48–50)

Strommen and Hardel, the authors of this study, offer the following comment about these results: "This study, just like Search Institute's first study done in 1960, reveals that both youth and parents want to communicate with one another on issues that are more than superficial. Youth prefer to discuss their problems and concerns with their parents rather than their peer group" (p. 50). They go on to say, "In spite of this declared interest in communicating with one's parents on sensitive issues, again only a minority of youth reports that this actually happens" (p. 50).

Craig Allan is the youth ministry coordinator at Saint Bernadette Parish in Seattle, Washington. In the spring of 2002, he polled the youth of his parish with these two questions:

- If you could have a conversation with anyone, who would it be?

- Whom do you have a hard time communicating with?

According to Allan 75 percent of youth indicated *parents* as their answer to both questions, which, of course, confirms the Search Institute study.

When one of the Search Institute researchers, Merton Strommen, met with a group of young people and asked them to identify what they deemed necessary for communication to be established in their home, the young people came up with three suggestions for parents:

1. Take time to share ideas and listen to what we have to say.
2. Initiate discussions using current world events. Such discussions will build a bridge of communication over which religious subjects can more easily move.
3. Give us the freedom to disagree with you and to hold a position that differs from yours.

This third suggestion was given with some feeling. The young people wanted the freedom to explore various positions in order to arrive at a position they could feel was theirs. (*Passing On the Faith,* p. 51)

Practical Application for Effective Youth Ministry

At Saint Bernadette's Craig Allan followed up his survey about parent-teen communication with a series of youth-group sessions in which the teens reflected on their future, their family life desires, and their current relationships with parents. The sessions concluded with a parent panel discussion.

In addition to the questions Allan used to poll the teens, he also asked the youth to reflect on their future family life by imagining they are twenty years older than they are today, and then responding to these questions:

• Are you married?

• How many children do you have?

• What are their ages and gender?

• In what ways are you raising your children as you were raised?

• In what ways are you raising your children differently than you were raised?

• Are you willing to share your responses with others in the youth group?

• Are you willing to share your responses with your parents?

Those questions prompted such animated discussion in the youth group that Allan knew the opportunity was ripe to bring parents in. The parents joined the following week. The process that Allan devised for the discussion allowed both the teens and parents to offer advice to each other. Again the discussion was animated and rich with meaning and emotion.

It is perhaps normal for teens, when gathered, to complain about their parents. The same may be true for parents about their teens. But when gathered together in a setting like Saint Bernadette's youth program, "suddenly everyone can see the power and depth of the parent-teen relationship," says Allan.

Allan maintains that teenagers need "a safe place to be, and, for a time, be separate, allowing them to discover themselves and mature." The youth group ought to be such a place. But on occasion, if the groundwork is done well—in this case reflecting on parent-teen relationships—separation can be replaced with union, leading to extraordinary growth.

Allan's work at Saint Bernadette's is a prime example of how a youth minister can be a catalyst for growth and can empower teens and their parents to form that key relationship. Part of teen development involves separation from parents. (How do I figure out what's me that isn't them?) However, the bond between parents and teens supercedes and transcends the developmental growth elements at play.

Questions to Ponder

What do you think of Craig Allan's notion that youth need a "safe place to be, and . . . be separate" and that the youth group ought to be such a place?

What role do parents play in this need for separation?

What could you do in your program to invite youth to reflect upon and discuss their relationships with their parents?

What could you do in your program to bring parents and youth together for discussion and mutual learning?

How might your youth ministry program be a catalyst for enhancing the relationship between parents and teens?

Chapter 4

Understanding Parents of Teens

Several times a year, I have the privilege of facilitating a workshop for middle school students and their parents. Recently I was at a parish in California with a group of about fifty parents and kids. At one point in the workshop, I had participants separated into family groups. The groups were scattered about the room, and I gave them a specific task to perform: Using only a short stack of newspapers and a roll of masking tape, each family was to build a table that would support a gallon jug of water (approximately 14 pounds). I instructed them to design the table in such a way that the gallon jug could also pass underneath it. Families were given 12 minutes to perform the task, and as an added challenge, I told them to work in silence for the first 3 minutes.

I have conducted this exercise often with groups of parents and teens, and most families do very well and succeed with their table. It's a great boost to their morale because it at first appears to be an impossible task. On this particular day, however, I noticed a mom and her two sons having a very difficult time. They were working furiously to beat the 12-minute time limit, but clearly they could not agree with one another on the design of their table and how to proceed. Consequently, what one person put together, another dismantled. All three were frustrated, and the mother was clearly embarrassed. I felt embarrassed too because I wanted the exercise to be a positive experience for families. I wanted to help them, rescue them. I have seen enough of these newspaper tables now to know just how to put one together quickly. But I knew if I even went near them, I would only add to their shame.

I should mention that when families walk in the door for this workshop, I usually see reticent and reluctant expressions on their faces—teens and parents alike. They do not know what to expect, but they are pretty sure it is not going to be much fun. I noticed the mother and two sons, and they certainly had those facial expressions when they came in the door.

So up to this point, from my view anyway, this particular family was not having a good time. While I was disappointed, I told myself that I could not please everyone, and that it wouldn't be that big of a deal if there were one poor evaluation sheet at the end of the workshop. Wouldn't be the first time.

Later in the workshop, I put participants in family groups again, spread throughout the room. This time their task was to engage in a structured conversation about the specific strengths of their family and how those strengths can help them deal with the stresses of being an adolescent family. These conversations are often deep and heartfelt. I looked over and saw a mother and her thirteen-year-old son holding hands while talking.

When I looked over to the mom with the two sons, I noticed that they too were into it heavy-duty. They did not look happy or intimate, but it was clear they were dealing with some of their issues head-on. I wanted to eavesdrop, though that wasn't necessary. I could get the gist of what was being said just by watching. Let me describe what I saw, and you can discern the meaning.

The two boys sat there with a posture of "attitude." Occasionally one or the other would roll his eyes. At first Mom was holding the discussion-guide sheet, and her gaze moved back and forth between the boys and the sheet while she talked. She wasn't getting much response. Finally she put the page aside, leaned forward, looked them both in the eye and spoke to them. Her face was sincere but stern. A pause. Then both boys started talking at once. She gestured at one; he spoke and she leaned in to hear. Then she did the same with the other. This pattern continued for several minutes. None of them was smiling, but they were covering some important ground. It was clear to me that this was a moment when Mom needed to sacrifice her popularity or camaraderie with her sons to say what needed to be said and to deal with important concerns. I very much admired this mom. After being embarrassed by the table-building activity, she was able to ignore the intimate family moments happening around her and focus her full attention and love on her sons and the current issues of their family. It was not fun or easy. Her boys did not like her very much at the moment, but she held her ground. It was a powerful expression of parental love.

Being a parent of a teenager becomes more challenging with each generation. The pace of life only increases; relationships only become more complex. Key moments arise, always unannounced and seldom anticipated, when a parent is challenged to be completely present, to shrug off the temptation of denial, and to face the issue head-on. I fear that today's parents are missing too many of these moments.

What the Numbers Show

Is there a difference between parents of teens today and parents of teens a generation ago? The statistics may give us a few insights, but a couple stories may also help answer the question.

When I was fifteen years old and a sophomore in high school (1973–1974), I had two siblings also in high school and a younger sister in her first year of middle school. We were a teenage family with *four* teenagers! How many families do you know today that have four teens? But what was truly phenomenal about our family was that we were not in the least extraordinary. The Webbers up the street had a handful of teens in the house for at least ten years running, as did the Lannons and the Kinskys. It was *normal* to have four or more children in the family.

Even a few short years later, when my wife and I took over at the Youth House at Saint Patrick's Parish in Spokane, many of the teens in the youth group came from very large families. In thinking about those families, I realized that the teens from those families who were part of the youth group were either the youngest or near the youngest child in the family. I cannot recall one teen from our Saint Pat's days who was the oldest in the family and who had at least three younger siblings.

As the '70s waned, so did the abundance of large families. In fact, a March 2000 U.S. Census Bureau report says that just over 70 percent of American families with children ages twelve to seventeen have only one child. The percentage of teenage families with three or more children is a mere 4.4 percent.

The percentage of children living in single-parent households has risen substantially. According to the Web site Unmarried America, in 1960 just 9 percent of children under age eighteen lived in a single-parent household. By 1980 that figure had risen to over 19 percent, and by 2000 nearly 27 percent of American children were living in a single-parent home.

Without joining the debate over whether a single-parent household is more or less detrimental to a child's upbringing than a two-parent household, it is undeniable that single parenting presents many extraordinary challenges to the *parent* that only makes the parent's job more difficult. Tasks like planning meals; managing time; dealing with finances; juggling job, home maintenance, and school issues; providing parental support; driving the kids to school and activities; and so on, all contribute to the stress and strain of single parenting.

Of course many single parents handle all those tasks, and much more, with extraordinary agility. And many other parents in two-parent homes (usually the mothers) are left juggling all those tasks on their own. A lot of single parenting occurs in two-parent homes. I must also point out that many parents parent better, and their children thrive more, in a single-parent setting than in a home where the two parents are highly contentious toward each other.

Another factor that makes today's parents of teens different from those of the previous generation is the high percentage of mothers who are employed outside the home. I grew up in a milieu that portrayed the typical American family as a working father whose salary was sufficient to sustain the family, a stay-at-home mom, a couple kids, a dog, and a station wagon. I grew up believing this was the norm, even though reality dictated otherwise. For most of my childhood, my parents ran their own small business, resulting in many long hours for my father and nearly full-time work for my mother. Much to my mother's credit, I grew up believing our family fit the typical American model, when in fact the nearly full-time employment of *both* my parents was crucial to our survival.

In 2000 the U.S. Census Bureau reported that the percentage of children growing up with both parents in some stage of employment has risen steadily in past decades. The Family Education Network reports that in 1850 women made up 13 percent of all paid workers in America. By 1900 that percentage had risen to 19, and by 1950 it had risen to 30. According to 2000 Census data, today in Nebraska nearly 70 percent of kids have both parents in the workforce. Jerry Deichert, director of the Center for Public Affairs Research at the University of Nebraska at Omaha, says the struggling farm economy may be forcing both parents to work. That statistic brings into question the widely held romantic myth that rural and small-town settings are better and easier places to raise a healthy family.

Statistics also show an increasing delay in marriage and child rearing. The Family Education Network reports that in 1998 the

median age for a woman's first marriage was twenty-five, up almost a
full five years since the early 1960s. Today more women are either
postponing or not ever having children. In 1995 nearly 27 percent of
women ages thirty to thirty-four had never given birth, compared to
16 percent in 1976. One contributing factor is the educational
attainment levels of women, which in 1998 exceeded those of men: 90
percent of women ages twenty-five to twenty-nine had at least a high
school diploma, and 29 percent had at least a bachelor's degree. The
respective percentages for men were 87 percent and 26 percent. Gone
are the days when women were sent off to college with the primary
purpose of finding a husband.

Parents Today

"Parents don't want to make their kids do anything," remarks Ann
LaBeck, a twenty-seven-year youth ministry veteran from Saint
Madeleine-Sophie Parish in Bellevue, Washington. St. Mad's—
as the locals call it—lies in the middle of an upper-middle-class
suburban community near the campus of Microsoft and other high-
tech corporations, just east of Seattle. "In most families both parents
are working full-time. Kids have much less one-to-one supervision
from their parents today," says LaBeck. She maintains that one of the
problems between parents and kids today is that they simply do not
spend enough time together. On limited time parents are trying to
make friends with and build relationships with their teens; therefore,
parents are reluctant to do the hard work of parenting that might
involve unpopular decisions. According to LaBeck, "When parents are
always trying to be their kids' buddies, they have trouble establishing
priorities and determining what's negotiable and what's nonnegotiable.
We need to give parents permission and support for being parents."

In her book *They're Your Kids, Not Your Friends,* Shirlee Smith
reflects on her days growing up in a working-class neighborhood in
Los Angeles: "Back then when nothing seemed to make much sense,
there was one thing that stood clear. That one thing was my family's

belief that children were to be taught a set of values, and those values were to be the cornerstone of our existence" (p. 13). The family and neighborhood community attempted to teach those values, and, says Smith, "the adults didn't care whether they were considered friend or foe. Back then adults knew they had a responsibility, and they carried it out with blatant disregard for popular ratings. . . . The most important disappearance from the old neighborhood structure are those behavior codes our parents, grandparents, and everyone else we were in contact with made us adhere to" (pp. 14–15).

In response to this struggle, LaBeck describes a simple strategy of regularly putting kids and parents in the same room to discuss such topics as communication, parent-teen relationships, and the like. When the youth ministry program creates the opportunity for those gatherings, parents and kids have time together in a "safe" place, which helps them understand each other's role in the family and allows all to see a host of models for how to be an adolescent family.

You might be interested in a couple workshops offered by Saint Mary's Press that are designed to accomplish the same purpose. "Welcoming the Teen Years: THRIVING, Not Just Surviving" is an experience for middle school students and their parents. "Prepare to Launch!" is a workshop for high school seniors and their parents. Many parishes and schools around the country have sponsored these workshops as part of their effort to partner with parents. For more information, visit *www.smp.org* or call 800-533-8095.

Practical Application for Effective Youth Ministry

The focus of this chapter is understanding parents. I have shared some of my own experiences and some broad statistics that together paint a general picture of today's parents of teens. But only you can get to know the parents of your community. Statistically what can you learn about the parents of teens in your parish? How old are they? How many are employed outside the home? How many have children who are either pre- or postadolescents? How many are single parents? divorced? remarried? Using parish and local census data, see if you can develop a statistical portrait of the teenage families in your community. What does the portrait tell you? What are the unique characteristics of parents in your area? How might this portrait influence your youth ministry programming?

How might you help parents lay claim to their role and responsibilities, their vocation as parents? The answer does not necessarily mean adding more programming. In fact, that is probably not the best move and certainly should not be your first move. Instead, begin with relationship building. Get to know as many parents as you can. Affirm them, and affirm their teens. Imagine yourself in a quasi-matchmaking role. As you get to know parents and the issues they are dealing with, look for ways to connect them with other parents who are confronting similar issues or concerns. If, for example, you know a family who has negotiated a teenage problem (drugs, poor grades, curfew, and so on), can you match them up with a parent who finds himself or herself in a similar situation? Let the strength of your personal relationship with both families be the bridge where the two of them can meet.

Similarly imagine the youth ministry program as a vehicle for parental support and networking. While kids will band together to make plans and engage in their activities, many parents feel isolated and unsure where to draw the boundaries. Through various communication channels like e-mail and phone lists, you might be able to make it easier for parents to connect with one another and work in concert with one another.

For parents whose teens attend a Catholic high school, give them a copy of *Parents and Schools in Partnership: A Message for Parents on Nurturing Faith in Teens* (Winona, MN: Saint Mary's Press, 2003). This small booklet (sixteen pages) explores in practical terms how the Catholic high school and family can be partners in effective faith formation of teens with respect to their learning about God, growing in relationship with God, and learning to respond to the needs of others.

Questions to Ponder

What do you think of Ann LaBeck's comment, "When parents are always trying to be their kids' buddies, they have trouble establishing priorities and determining what's negotiable and what's nonnegotiable. *We need to give parents permission and support for being parents*"? Do you agree or disagree? Why?

Of all the challenges facing parents of teens today, which do you consider the most difficult? Why? What might the parish and the community do to help parents address that challenge?

Of the parents of teens you know, bring to mind one or two whom you believe are doing a great job. Why did you choose them? What positive characteristics do they show? How might you help other parents acquire those characteristics?

Chapter 5

Sorting Through the Baggage

A teen reminisces with his sister on the eve of her going off to college:

> The last night my sister was home we sat up and talked about stuff, like when we were little, what we remembered, and what we'll miss now that she's going to college. All of sudden I felt like crying, and I held it in. But then I looked over at Lindsay and she *was* crying, and then we *both* cried. (Patricia Pasick, *Almost Grown,* pp. 154–155)

Another teen reflects on the changing behavior of her father as she grows and matures:

> My Dad was regressing a little. He started holding my arm as we were crossing a busy street, and giving me exact directions how to find a bookstore that was in plain view across the street. The last straw (but I loved it): he dashed into a shop and bought a Kermit puppet for me. (P. 78)

Another teen senses the angst between himself and his parents as they all prepare for his departure to college.

Parents shouldn't make kids more nervous and anxious than they already are. At my house my Mom keeps saying, "What am I going to do when you're gone?" My answer: The same thing *I'm* going to do at school: Live a life! Leaving home for the first time is stressful enough without people telling you that they are going to miss you. (P. 149)

The Invisible Bag

Imagine that on the day you were born, among many other gracious treasures and gifts, you were given an invisible bag. Imagine that you have been carrying that bag over your shoulder since day one. What's the purpose of the bag? To store important stuff, of course. Since the day you were born, people, usually the important ones like parents, family members, friends, siblings, and so on, have been putting things in your bag—not physical things but real things nonetheless.

The key people in your life have stuffed your bag with beliefs, expectations, behaviors, prejudices, responsibilities, roles, rules, even feelings and emotions. To a greater or lesser degree, the stuff in your bag governs the way you live your life. Don't worry. Over the years you've done your share of stuffing others' bags also. You see, *everyone* has a bag, and whenever we get close to people, we tuck a few things into theirs.

Every so often your bag gets a bit heavy, so you pull it off your shoulder and do some sorting. Psychologically this is a very healthy activity, although often quite disturbing to those key people who have been stuffing your bag. There are moments when you reach into the bag, pull out a few items, hold them up, and make a choice: Keep or toss? The experts call this process self-differentiation. A parent watching a precocious twenty-month-old baby sorting for the first time calls this the terrible twos. I call it just sorting through our baggage.

As you might imagine, it's natural to do some sorting at certain times in your life. Think about it: When do you naturally clean out and organize your physical stuff? Usually just prior to or during times of change and transition, right? You have a yard sale to get rid of stuff before moving to a new home (change). You clean out, spruce up, and paint that little room next your bedroom to make a space for the new baby (major change). You clean out and organize the garage to make room for the boat you've always dreamed of owning (fun change).

You also sort through your invisible baggage just prior to and during times of change and transition. I already mentioned the terrible twos as a natural sorting moment. That is when baby begins to realize that there is a whole part of "me" that isn't Mommy. A couple key sorting words that baby uses are, of course, "NO!" and "MINE!"

What are some other natural moments of change and transition that might lead a person to sort through his or her baggage? Consider times like going off to school, entering adolescence, high school graduation, and leaving home as a young adult.

One of the most interesting times of sorting occurs when a couple are engaged to be married. It is both natural and necessary for them to do some sorting in preparation for a lifelong, covenantal commitment to each other. The couple may find themselves trying to resist the temptation to tuck at least a few important values, beliefs, expectations, roles, and so on, into each other's bag! Parents and in-laws also have trouble resisting the temptation.

Let's take an in-depth look at adolescence as a profound time for baggage sorting. Putting myself into teenager shoes, I realize that I naturally want to figure out what about me is distinct from my parents, my family, their expectations, beliefs, rules, roles, and responsibilities. When I reach into my bag to reflect on what to keep and what to toss, I pull out items that hold great meaning and emotional power with my parents. I demand to hold those items up and to be given the opportunity to observe and reflect upon all facets before I decide to keep them and own them for myself or toss them and leave them behind with childhood. (What I don't know at the time, as a teenager, is that even if I toss an item, that little piece of baggage may linger with me for many years yet, and it may even be part of future sortings.)

Here's an example: As I'm writing this chapter, it is early October and my seventeen-year-old son is preparing his essay for his college applications, which are due soon. The topic of his essay is faith. He writes how faith is important to his parents and how he has been raised in a family that practices faith and worships regularly. He expresses admiration for his parents. But he goes on to explain that as he has given his Catholic upbringing and formation much consideration, he simply cannot embrace what the Catholic Church stands for and teaches.

Am I sad that he has taken that posture? A little, but I'm not devastated. Clearly he has done a lot of searching, reflecting, perhaps even praying, so I know he is engaged in the spiritual journey. God lingers in the creases and folds of my son's daily life, and I'm comforted in knowing that my son is on the lookout for God. How could I not be honored that my son would share his essay with me, knowing full well that he and I are seemingly parting ways spiritually? His essay has made for fascinating faith conversation at our table.

This is a classic and common example of adolescent sorting. When you think about the youth and parents with whom you work and minister, generally faith and religious practice are important aspects of their lives. If faith and religious practice weren't important to them, you would not have the opportunities to interact with these youth and parents. Therefore, it is not surprising that as teenagers reach into their bag to do a little sorting, they often pull out the very things their parents, families, and youth minister want them to keep and take with them as they launch into young adulthood. But remember, their sorting is necessary and healthy. Imagine the alternative. If they never raised up faith and religious practice—just left those in the bag and didn't give them any real thought or reflection—what good would that do? So what if they *automatically* go to Mass at the Newman Center at college? If they don't have any sense of personal ownership, personal relationship, it's as if faith were never in the bag in the first place.

The natural sorting process tells you something about how you need to catechize teenagers. If your faith formation program does not allow them openness and space to reach into their bag, hold up faith and religious practice, examine all facets of their faith, ask a lot of questions, express doubts, and *reach their own conclusions,* then you are doing them a disservice.

Just one more thought on this sorting business. Keep in mind that it is not only teens who are rummaging through their bags deciding what to keep and what to toss but also their parents. Many parents of teenagers find themselves on the cusp of midlife, which also presents a natural moment for sorting. I address this notion in greater detail in the next chapter, but for now we should recognize that it is not unusual for a lot of sorting and questioning to occur in a typical adolescent family. Makes life interesting!

On the Front Lines of Ministry

Maryelyn Scholz has been the youth ministry coordinator at Saint Vincent de Paul Parish in Federal Way, Washington, for the past eight years. She had twenty years of ministry under her belt before coming to Saint Vincent's. "Kids don't live in a vacuum," says Scholz. "Most of them live in families. The more we connect with those families, resource their parents, the more effective we can be with the teens." Scholz sees herself as a partner with parents in *their* efforts to raise good kids, form them in their faith, and launch them into young adulthood with confidence and maturity. As a mother of teens herself, she puts as much energy into building relationships with parents as she does teens. "I just try to love them—kids, parents, everyone."

In her efforts to love them—kids, parents, everyone—Scholz has found herself journeying through some tough times with kids and their families. A recent teen pregnancy is just one example. When she took the initiative to reach out to the pregnant girl's mother with a phone call, the mother's reticent shame quickly dissolved into tears, and eventually gratitude. "Look at your role," says Scholz. "It's to help kids, right? Kids are part of a family. When I become visible in everyone's life, I'm in a position to help those who can really help the kids. Most often that's the parents." Scholz knew that the help she could give to the pregnant teenager could only go so far as long as the teen and her mother were at odds. In reaching out to the girl's mother, Scholz was a catalyst for allowing the mother and daughter to make a difficult and painful journey *together.* Smart ministry.

As kids sort through the baggage of adolescence, they need more than their parents as significant adults in their lives. "Children need a network of adults with whom to relate: parents of peers, single persons, married persons without children, older adults, both kin and nonkin. Such a network provides a child with security, respite from parents and additional life model" (*Family Ministry,* p. 560).

A study of 5,000 fourth through twelfth graders conducted in the early 1990s and sponsored by the Girl Scouts found, not surprisingly, that young people are most likely to turn to their parents for advice. After their parents they will turn to relatives and adults with whom they have regular contact. In the March 1992 *RespecTeen* newsletter, Eugene C. Roehlkepartain reports:

> Search Institute research supports this finding, noting that young people most often turn to adults when facing major life choices (though they likely ask their peers about day-to-day concerns such as fashions, appearance, and dating). Furthermore, as young people mature, non-related adults become more significant sources of support, guidance, and modeling" *(www.search-institute.org/archives/wtnfa.htm).* Unfortunately, though, many teenagers don't have access to caring adults. In the *RespecTeen*-sponsored study, *The Troubled Journey: A Portrait of 6th–12th Grade Youth,* Search Institute found that only 49 percent of young people have non-parent adults they can turn to for advice and support. Furthermore, just 42 percent of kids say they have frequent, in-depth conversations with non-parent adults.

Clearly Maryelyn Scholz is one of those significant adults in the lives of many teens, providing a valuable ministry and service to them. Yet Scholz has an even broader vision for people involved in youth ministry. "Parents have the influence to steer their kids toward positive significant adults," she says. "Parents always have more influence over their kids than I do." If Scholz can help the parents, nurturing them in their parental vocation, she knows she's helping the ones who have the most impact on kids.

Sorting Causes Problems

Earlier in this chapter, I glibly mentioned that when you sort through your bag, those around you, those who love you, those who have made concerted efforts to put things into your bag, can become anxious and agitated. What will you do with the precious pieces they inserted— toss or keep? I also mentioned that teenagers sort through the items that mean the most to their parents and family. In some families the natural sorting process for teens (and for midlife parents) combined with all the other activities, distractions, and stressors of hectic family life can result in serious problems for one or more family members, such as teen pregnancy, poor grades, dropping out of school, marital strife, divorce, substance abuse, physical abuse, and so on. Those problems can be very complicated, making it difficult to pinpoint exact causes in any given family struggle.

While normal, natural, and developmental, sorting through one's bag, particularly at the adolescent stage, can be dangerous. Merton Strommen and Richard Hardel, authors of *Passing On the Faith: A Radical New Model for Youth and Family Ministry,* maintain that the congregation must play an important role in helping families do their sorting, especially if they run into problems: "[The congregation] is the one organization whose purpose and message is to affect close family relationships; it is the one place where parents can experience the redemption found in a personal relationship with God" (p. 37).

Similar to the approach Maryelyn Scholz took with the family of
a pregnant teen, Strommen and Hardel support a personal, relational,
pastoral approach to helping families deal with serious problems and
strengthen their relationships. In their book *Passing On the Faith,* they
summarize the following pastoral suggestions, which emerged from a
survey of families in southern California:

- Personal contact is most effective. Assistance with child care, calls
  on the telephone, or home visits are especially appreciated.
- Support groups are essential. Ninety-three percent of the survey
  respondents say the church should provide support groups for
  people experiencing crises.
- Family training seminars help. Seminars that focus on family
  crises and equip individuals to communicate better are highly
  recommended.
- Pastoral counseling is helpful, but 92 percent of the respondents
  felt that pastors [and others on the pastoral team] should be
  trained to be more effective in counseling.
- Printed material has limited effectiveness. Though viewed to be
  of some value, such materials are least effective in achieving
  personal healing.

(Summarized from Fred Kasischke and Audray Johnson,
"Mything the Point, Dealing with Denial, Getting the Facts")

According to Strommen and Hardel, the authors of those suggesions
"indicate that healing takes place when family crises are openly
acknowledged, when families feel supported in a caring group setting,
when families experience concrete acts of love and concern, and when
all efforts are bathed in prayer" (*Passing On the Faith,* p. 46).

Practical Application for Effective Youth Ministry

Your church may be an ideal setting for intergenerational contact.
According to Eugene C. Roehlkepartain:

Church is one of the few places where people of all ages can regularly interact together. However, many churches segregate ages in their programs so that youth group members never have contact with anyone outside the group. Here are things churches can do to build bridges:

1. Have intergenerational programs. These might include special classes or workshops, or even an ongoing intergenerational Sunday school class. These experiences can become a foundation for adults becoming significant supporters of teenagers.

2. Highlight the experiences and needs of young people in sermons and other public settings to help adults stay aware of needs and issues.

3. Offer classes and workshops that help adults learn listening and other skills so they'll be more comfortable with teenagers.

4. Include young people in visible leadership positions in the church. They'll not only contribute to the church's ministry, but they'll have more opportunities to interact with adults.

5. Sponsor mentor programs that pair an adult in the congregation with a teenager who's interested in a particular field. Or have adults offer tutoring and support to young people who particularly need it.

("What Teens Need from Adults")

Questions to Ponder

Does your youth ministry encourage better communication among parents and between parents and teens? How can you help both teens and their parents do their necessary sorting?

How do you address the fact that communication in the home decreases as children approach adolescence? How can you help teens discuss issues with their parents?

Does your ministry stress the importance of families demonstrating love and affection for one another? How do you encourage emotional bonding between parents and teens? How can you help parents overcome a tendency to express less affection as their children grow older?

Chapter 6

The Internal Walkman

I enjoy the privilege of working from home. As an editor for Saint Mary's Press, I work out of my home office, in Portland, Oregon, while the company headquarters is based in Winona, Minnesota. It's a great arrangement. My "office" is actually in the family garage. A few years ago, my son and I remodeled a corner of the garage, installed a couple windows, hooked up electrical and phone lines, and created a very comfortable workspace.

One day not too long ago, I got up from my desk and went into the house to get a drink of water. As I was crossing the patio to the back door, I could hear excessive noise. When I got into the house, I could hear that the overpowering music and strong bass vibrations were coming from my younger son's room, down the hall from the kitchen. He had his favorite rock album blasting from his sound system while playing along on his own bass guitar, which was plugged into an amp the size of small car. Yikes!

I went upstairs in search of my older son. As I ascended the stairs, I began to feel a different rhythmic beat. In his room my older son was listening to his favorite Native American drumming music, which was emanating at full volume from his boom box, and keeping the beat with his own 3-foot-diameter drum!

Our house was rocking! Needless to say the boys' mother was not home. I got my drink of water and went back to my office, hoping my neighbor wouldn't see me over the back fence.

I came back to my office with just one question in mind: Why do teenagers need to play their music so loud at times? After dwelling on this question for awhile, I landed on a theory that, whether true or not, at least makes sense to me. It has to do with the internal Walkman that plays in their heads 24/7/365.

Questions

That's right. There is an internal Walkman playing in their heads all the time, and it does not play music. Instead it plays questions. In each teen's unique style, language, and rhythm, the internal Walkman is constantly asking questions like these:

- How do I look?

- Who am I, really?

- Who am I becoming?

- Who are the people who like me?

- Do I like them?

- Who are the people who love me?

- What am I going to do with my life?

- What about SEX?

- What about relationships?

- What am I going to eat?

- How do I look?

- What about SEX?

At times the volume on these questions is cranked so high that a teen simply cannot hear anything else. As a parent, I shake my head and

muse, "How can anyone be so self-absorbed?" That's exactly what it is
. . . *developmental*. At this stage in their lives, developmentally, teens
are grappling with so many unanswered questions that, for periods of
time, they cannot focus on anything or anyone other than themselves.
Maybe teenagers need to crank the music every so often just so they
can hear and enjoy something other than those darn questions.

Trying to drown out all the nagging questions is normal, natural,
and necessary behavior. Does that mean a parent should not ask a
teen to "TURN DOWN THAT MUSIC!"? Of course not. Because
families all live under the same roof, they have to figure out how to
live in harmony with one another. Yet if the parents understand that
some of this behavior is developmental and not pathological, then the
manner in which they handle the inevitable points of conflict may be
more up front and compassionate.

Sounds relatively simple, right? Parents can handle their teenager's internal Walkman behavior now that they know there's a reason
behind it, right? Actually, it's not so easy. Recall from chapter 5 that
many parents of teens find themselves on the cusp of that wonderful
developmental stage our society lovingly calls midlife. Guess what?
There's also an internal Walkman that plays in the head of midlifers,
24/7/365. This one too plays questions instead of music—questions
very similar to those your teenager's internal Walkman plays:

- How do I look?

- Do I still look okay?

- Who am I, really?

- Who have I become?

- Who are the people who like me?

- Do I like them?

- Who are the people who love me?

- What am I going to do with the rest of my life?

- What about SEX?

- What about relationships?

- What am I going to eat?

- What am I going to avoid eating?

- How do I look?

- What about SEX?

While teens are climbing up the mountain, and there is nothing but possibility in front of them, parents find themselves on the way down, and life's limitations are all too apparent. Occasionally the volume of the midlife Walkman gets pretty loud, making it a struggle for the parent to hear anything but those darn questions. So it wouldn't be unusual for a teenager to say something like: "Dad, you are so lame. What planet are you from?" (actual words heard in the Kehrwald household).

The adolescent family is developmentally pregnant with questions, and most of them go to the core of each member's identity. That leaves family members quite vulnerable, and they become ultrasensitive to the little remarks made by others, keying their daily dose of self-worth off external input that is usually made without much thought or sensitivity.

In her book *Family Ministry: A Comprehensive Guide*, Diana R. Garland summarizes these developmental challenges this way:

> Teenagers face the developmental tasks of establishing their own identity and launching their own career and, sooner or later, their own adult family. Their parents must provide them with a shifting combination of security, freedom and responsibility. At the same time, parents are dealing with their own developmental issues—midlife career and marital changes and the beginning signs of aging. In addition, their own parents may be increasingly in need of social support and, if they are frail, caregiving or other forms of assistance. . . .

. . . Families are . . . not the structures of relationships that last but processes that link one generational expression of family to the next. (P. 113)

Another factor at play in teenage families has to do with parents' realizing, often for the first time, that some of their lifelong personal dreams are *not* going to come true. As a forty-four-year-old, I have just about come to grips with the fact that I am not going to make the PGA tour. Even the senior tour looks doubtful. But sometimes the skewed logic of the Walkman might suggest to parents that, perhaps with a little nudging here and there, they might be able to get one of their young strapping teenagers to live out their dreams for them. After all, it just seems natural to raise children in the image and likeness of themselves. Yikes! I imagine you've seen this phenomenon.

I went to high school with a boy who was an outstanding baseball player. By senior year professional scouts were showing up at games to watch him pitch. But in the middle of baseball season of his senior year, he quit the team, saying, "Baseball just isn't for me." His dad was the coach of the baseball team and had been his baseball coach ever since T-ball days. And wouldn't you know, the dad, as a young ballplayer himself, had come close to making it to the big leagues. The son was living Dad's dream, not his own.

The term *internal Walkman* is simply one way to describe the core developmental tasks of teenagers and their parents. Most youth ministry programs account well for the developmental issues of teens but often are not cognizant of many of the same issues prevalent in parents.

Parish Perspective

Betty Jo Levad (she goes by B. J.) is parish pastoral minister at Holy Family Church in Yakima, Washington. She has worked in the parish for many years and is a fixture of the community. She has raised her own children at Holy Family, which means that all those years she has worked with parents and kids she was also raising her own children. "Kids come with parents. It's that simple," says Levad. "Here at Holy

Family we have gone through an attitude change from protecting kids from their parents to partnering with parents. Reaching out to parents is key to our ministry with kids."

Staff members at Holy Family recognize that teens and their parents have a lot more in common than may be evident at first glance, so the youth ministry leaders use a small-group structure in the program, which means a lot of adults are around to serve as mentors for the teens. Two adults are assigned to each small group of ten to twelve youth, and a number of those adults are parents. Sometimes a teen wants to be in the same group with his or her parent, sometimes not. In these small groups, parents and teens alike grow in relationship with each other, grow in their faith, and gain insights and skills for navigating life's challenges. Parents and teens learning and growing *together* creates an atmosphere in which parents and teens can talk with each other on deeper levels.

In addition to the small-group structure, B. J. recommends special social and service experiences for parents and teens together. Events such as mother-son or father-daughter dances and the like can be fun and powerful bonding experiences. B. J. also recommends support groups or networks for parents to "talk with each other and share ideas about raising their teens."

Practical Application for Effective Youth Ministry

The internal Walkman in the heads of teens and their parents can either hinder family relationships or enrich them. Of course it is in your best interest to help parents and teens enrich their relationships with each other. I believe that family well-being and family faith are linked. When family members spend time together, build healthy relationships with one another, share meals with one another, and solve conflicts and reconcile with one another, they grow not only in well-being but also in faith. When the internal Walkman of either the teen or the parent is blaring at high volume, it surely tests the relational qualities and skills of the entire family. It may lead to serious family struggle. But when families are able to absorb the blaring Walkman, surround the individual with love, solve their problems, and reconcile with one another, they become strengthened in their own identity and are empowered to face future challenges.

How can you, the youth minister, help? Two words: *skills* and *memories*. You can provide opportunities for adolescent families to sharpen their *skills* in communication, conflict management, values clarification, and family problem solving. You can create experiences for adolescent families to *remember* the paths they have traveled together and to garner the strength of their past shared experiences. You can do all this intergenerationally, in either gathered or non-gathered settings.

Let me offer two simple tools for you to adapt and use in your own programming.

A Five-Step Process for Addressing Family Conflict

In the workshop "Welcoming the Teen Years: THRIVING, Not Just Surviving," which I am a presenter for, I offer parents and young teens a simple model for family meetings to deal with family conflict. All families find themselves in conflict at some point. It's a natural, normal part of living together. It's a sign of strength when families take specific steps to address and resolve their conflicts. Other characteristics common among families who reconcile well include these:

- spending energy seeking solutions rather than placing blame
- distinguishing between the person and the act
- understanding the difference between excusing and forgiving (They simply excuse the excusable, but they do the hard work of forgiving and reconciling the inexcusable.)
- ritualizing and celebrating their healing

In the workshop I encourage families to use the following **five steps for communicating amidst their chaos and hurts:**

1. Set aside time together to specifically address the problem. If tempers are hot, wait awhile for things to cool down.

2. Seek understanding of the issues and the feelings behind them. Give each person a chance to talk without being interrupted.

3. Brainstorm solutions. Try to generate all possible ideas. Prioritize them and choose a solution that everyone can live with.

4. Do it—practice the solution.

5. Evaluate and celebrate. Set aside time to discuss whether the solution is working. If it is, reward yourselves! If it isn't, go through the five steps again.

If you plan to have parents and teens gathered, you could design a simple session like this one:

1. Using small-group and large-group discussion, identify typical issues that cause teenage family conflict.

2. Through a brief content presentation, use the analogy of the internal Walkman to offer some input on adolescent families.

3. Create an attractive handout that lists the five steps for addressing family conflict. You might also include the characteristics common among families who heal and reconcile. Invite families to practice the five steps in small groups by role-playing a few of the causes of teenage family conflict identified earlier. For this role-play, ask parents and teens to switch roles. That makes it more fun!

4. Send families home with the five-step handout, encouraging them to use it or adapt it to their own personalities when necessary.

Remembering and Moving On

This activity is best used with older teens (juniors and seniors) and their parents. It can be quite powerful, especially when the family is on the verge of change, such as high school graduation or launching a son or daughter off to college, into the military, or into the workforce.

1. Recollection

- Invite participants to reflect, remember, and write about a special moment shared between parent and child. Have them bring to mind a moment of meaning, an unforgettable experience, or a profound event that the two of them shared together. Bring to mind the positives, negatives, losses, and gains.

- Invite participants to share the memories and stories with each other in family groups.

- Have some instrumental music playing in the background while participants share in family groups.

2. For Parents

- Invite the parents to stand. Ask the teens to remain seated quietly for the next few minutes.

- Ask the parents to close their eyes and imagine they are standing at the door of their son or daughter's bedroom, peering inside. Pause for about 30 seconds.

- Invite the parents to silently reflect on these questions:
  - What memories are evoked when you peer into your teen's room?
  - As your teen launches into young adulthood, what do you hope he or she takes with him or her?
  - What feelings come over you?

3. For Teens

- Invite the teens to stand and face their parents. Give them a moment just to gaze into each other's eyes.

- Invite the teens to reflect on these questions:
  - What have you learned from this parent?
  - What values, gifts, qualities, and lessons will you take with you as you launch into young adulthood?

4. For Parents and Teens

- Now, ask the parents and the teens to turn away from each other, toward the world, and have them reflect on this question:
  - Parents: In what ways are you called or challenged to let go? In what ways are you hoping to stay connected?
  - Teens: What draws you, calls you, taps your passions for making a difference in the world?

5. Write

- Invite participants to recall their responses to the reflection questions and to spend some time in further reflection and writing about what feelings, images, and observations have been evoked by this exercise.

6. Sharing in Family Groups

- Invite participants to share with each other in family groups.

7. Large-Group Comments (brief)

- Invite anyone in the group to share a comment with the whole group. If need be, stimulate a few comments by asking these general questions:
  - What surprised you in this process?
  - What insights, or pearls of wisdom, do you have that the rest of us could benefit from?
  - What are you glad you thought of?

8. Conclusion

- Conclude with remarks similar to these:

  Just as you stand at the threshold of young adult life, Jesus, too, once stood at a threshold. This threshold, the beginning of his public mission, was marked by the affirmation of his unique relationship with his Father as Jesus was baptized by John in the Jordan River: "On coming up out of the water he saw the heavens being torn open and the Spirit, like a dove, descending upon him.

And a voice came from the heavens, 'You are my beloved Son; with you I am well pleased.'" (Mark 1:10–11)

Following his baptism "the Spirit drove him out into the desert" (Mark 1:12), where he fasted and was tempted by Satan.

In the desert temptations, Jesus faced a basic choice about the direction of his life: Would he depend on his own power or on his Father's constant love for him? Each of us faces a similar choice as we stand at the great thresholds of our lives. As we face times of conflict and change, will we rely only on ourselves, or will we trust in God's constant love for us?

Questions to Ponder

When you were a teenager, what were two or three of the most prominent questions playing on your internal Walkman? What are a few of the prominent questions playing now?

Of the teens you know, what are two or three of the most prominent questions playing on their internal Walkman? In your relational, pastoral ministry with them, what might you do to help ease their anxieties and turn down the volume?

Of the parents of teens you know, bring to mind one parent who you believe handles the developmental issues of his or her teen quite well. What personal characteristics and skills do you see in this parent? List them. Can you think of ways to invite other parents to incorporate those characteristics and skills into their parenting?

Chapter 7

Change, Conversion, and Family Resistance

I grew up in a small town, attended a Catholic grade school, and went to Sunday Mass just about every week. I was a typical Catholic kid in our town—no more or less religious than anybody else. After my ninth-grade year, I received a great opportunity to attend a somewhat elite prep school in northern California. This boarding school, which was within walking distance of the ocean, was nestled among some of the world's best golf courses. Because golf was my passion, I leapt at the opportunity, spending the remainder of my high school career at Robert Louis Stevenson School, an all-boys, private, nonsectarian college prep school.

Early in my senior year, Robin, a girl I liked, who attended the neighboring girls' school, invited me and my buddies to attend her youth group. We agreed to go, and she told us she would pick us up the following Wednesday evening. When Wednesday rolled around, I went to round up my friends, but each had a seemingly lame excuse for why he couldn't go. I felt abandoned, but I liked Robin and decided to go with her without my buddies.

The youth group was unlike anything I had ever experienced in a "religious" setting. People were so welcoming. We had a lot of fun singing, playing games, creating skits, and so on. The religious message was simple: Jesus seeks a personal relationship with me. You might say the message was simplistic, but it hit home with me at that moment in my life. I was raised Catholic, so of course I was a believer. I even continued to go to Mass when I was away at school. But my personal faith took a huge leap forward that year, all because I decided to participate in Robin's youth group throughout my senior year. Eventually I convinced my buddies from school to come along, and they had a great time as well. I'm not sure they all had a "conversion" experience, but I certainly did.

My participating in this youth group changed me in ways that surprised some folks. I no longer partied. I read the Bible daily. I talked about God with just about anyone who would care to listen. I helped out with service efforts both on and off campus. The letters I wrote home to my folks changed. I told them what I was doing and how I was feeling and growing in my faith. Their response was supportive but tepid. I later learned from my brother that my parents were actually quite concerned about this "youth group" I was involved with. It was not Catholic, so it was suspect. I was changing in positive ways, but my folks did not know how to handle it.

Families Are Complicated

Is it pretty safe to presume that in your ministry with youth, whatever good comes to the young person will automatically have a positive impact on his or her family?

Recall what I wrote in chapter 3 about myths: A myth is something that has enough credibility to be believed but not enough to be true. The presumptuous statement that whatever good comes to the young person will automatically have a positive impact on the family is a myth. In many instances the statement may indeed hold up. A young person joins a youth program, makes some friends, learns a bit about his faith, begins to participate in other church activities. The parents are happy, there is less tension between parent and teen, and all is good. My presumptuous statement holds true . . . on a *behavioral* level.

Family dynamics, however, introduce a deeper, more complicated level. I am certainly not an expert in family process, but I can share with you a few things that have always made sense to me and that I believe are quite pertinent to ministry with youth.

In the 1980s author and speaker John Bradshaw popularized an image of the family as a mobile that hangs from the ceiling. (I believe the image was first coined a decade or two earlier by Virginia Satir.) Imagine each piece of the mobile representing one person in the family. All the pieces hang in delicate balance with one another. For the family this balance is what the experts call homeostasis, which is essentially the place at which we come to rest.

One difference to note right away is that when the mobile is balanced it is healthy. It is hanging just as it should. A family's balance is always a combination of good health and ill health, function and dysfunction. This balance is simply the natural resting place for the family, say, after a period of stress or excitement.

Think about the mobile for a moment. What happens when you bump one piece? All the other pieces move, right? The impact reverberates throughout the entire system. After a few moments, the mobile comes back to its resting place. For a family a "bump" to one person that reverberates throughout is actually a sign of health. Adolescence is filled with bumps, like accomplishments, disappointments, emotional outbursts, highs and lows. When those experiences are lived and absorbed by the entire family (as opposed to just the teen or just one other family member, such as Mom) the teen and the family as a whole maintain a healthier balance.

Think about the mobile again. What happens when you actually change the weight of just one piece of the mobile? The whole thing collapses, right? At this point what options do you have for correcting the problem and getting the mobile to hang? When I pose this question to groups, they often give me one of two responses: (1) change the weight of the other pieces, or (2) change the distance or relationship between the pieces. Both of those suggestions will lead to a *new* balance for the mobile. But there is a third option also: Remove the weight change from the original piece and return to the *old* balance.

You might now be recognizing the mythical nature of my earlier presumptuous statement about good for one person having a positive impact on the whole family. As a system of relationships, families naturally resist change. They prefer their existing balance, even when they recognize that a new balance may be better. Families prefer to live with chronic pain than to go through the acute pain of healing. This is especially true when the change is centered in just one member of the family.

Now think about your ministry with youth. When all is said and done, isn't helping young people to recognize God's gracious activity in their lives, to respond to it, and to grow into it what you're about in youth ministry? The religious word we use for this phenomenon is *conversion.* My conversion story that opens this chapter, when looked at from a systems viewpoint, is a story about *change,* and change is nearly always resisted.

Like the mobile, when one family member experiences change, all others must adjust, not necessarily experience the same change, in order for that change to be lasting. In other words the whole family must seek a *new* balance. The problem is that, as a system, the family will first attempt to exercise the third option, trying to change the individual back to the way he or she was before. Even if the initial change is a positive one, for instance faith conversion, the system will naturally resist because that seems easier than everyone having to adjust to the change. In the story about my conversion, I shared that my parents were outwardly supportive of my newfound personal relationship with Jesus but were privately concerned and worried.

Let me offer another example. Picture an average Catholic family with a more-or-less average teenage son. The parents have pushed pretty hard for their son to participate in the faith formation program at their parish. While the teen has pushed back, straining parent-teen relations, he has been attending the program. Fortunately for the teen and his family, they are members of *your* parish, and the teen is participating in *your* faith formation program. As a result of your relational, energetic, provocative, and, dare I say, fun program, this teen's resistance is diminishing, and he is becoming more engaged. He is learning about his faith. He is learning to pray and read the Scriptures. He is sensing God's gracious activity in his life and is beginning to respond. Needless to say, his parents are thrilled.

Now let's say it's time for your youth group to take its annual weekend retreat trip to the coast (or the mountains, or the desert, or wherever). The timing of this retreat is perfect for this young teen. He soaks it all in. He encounters Jesus the Christ in an intensely personal, powerful way. He catches a glimpse of his future as a person of God. He experiences *conversion,* well beyond anything he (or his parents) have imagined or experienced.

Late Sunday afternoon the youth-group van drops him in front of his house. On Friday afternoon when he left for the retreat, all was normal at home. A mere 48 hours later, he feels he's a different person. What will it be like for him to walk into his house and rejoin his family?

The teen has experienced something deeper than just a change in behavior, so his parents may say things like, "Wow, sounds like a truly powerful weekend. . . . Do you have much homework to finish up before school tomorrow?" Or they may just say, "Hmm . . . uhh . . . awesome," as though they want to be supportive but don't know how to go there with their son, don't know what to say, and so naturally seek familiar territory in which to relate. Can you sense the subtle resistance? Can you sense the desire to get back to normal? Will all families respond this way? No, and I address why in a moment. But as a system, the first natural inclination for a family confronted with change that upsets the balance is resistance and an effort to return to normalcy. To the extent that the change disrupts the balance, the family will resist it, even if it is positive.

We should not underestimate the power of the family system. Much of the very best ministry the Church does with individuals (teen retreats, adult encounters, catechumenate process, and so on) gets undone subconsciously by the family system, gently but surely, pulling the individual and the entire system back into its normal state. Does this happen in every case? No, but how often have you witnessed a young person's significant faith encounter, say, over a weekend retreat, and then several weeks later see no real difference in that young person's life? Or perhaps more common, how often do you witness a young person having such an encounter and then later going through a period of turmoil, strife, and confusion? Could it be that the young person's important relational systems (family, peer group, and so on) are resisting his or her change, and, the young person, feeling the conversion slip away, doesn't know what to do? How often have you heard your colleagues in RCIA ministry bemoan the fact that so few neophytes become active, regular attending members of the worshiping community? Could it be that both the neophytes' family systems *and* their worshipping community system have not made room for these new Christians?

Overcoming the Resistance to Change

The primary goal of youth ministry and youth faith formation is to help young people respond to God's gracious activity in their lives. The challenge is to help families adjust to the changes that occur in the lives of teens when youth ministry efforts do exactly what they are designed to do. Not all families resist the change of conversion and faith growth, because some have seen it before, have experienced it themselves, have an open posture toward change, understand the natural resistance, and have been able to anticipate the effects of change. You can help other families do much the same by making some simple adjustments in your ministry programming.

For six years Cathy Walz has participated in, and coordinated programs for, Young Neighbors in Action, a Catholic service-learning program for teams of older adolescents and adults, sponsored by the Center for Ministry Development. (For more information on Young Neighbors in Action, visit *www.youngneighbors.org*.) As a veteran youth minister and former eighth-grade teacher from Prospect Heights, Illinois (a Chicago suburb), Walz organizes groups of teens who spend a week in Mexico serving poor and needy communities. Teens often have a profound conversion experience that changes their lives, but they also commonly have a difficult time re-entering their home and family life after their conversion experience.

"When in Tijuana, we spend our days serving and working. Then we gather in the evenings to reflect on our service and make connections to Scripture and Catholic social teaching. We conclude each day with prayer," says Walz. One effort that Walz has made to connect parents and family members back home to the experience their teens are having in Mexico is an invitation for parents and family members to gather at the parish each evening to pray along with their teens. "I wrote up the prayer guide we use with the teens and leave it with the parents. They pray the same prayers and reflect on the same Scriptures as we do, at the same time. It's a powerful spiritual connection for both parents and teens."

When the youth group returns home, they host a gathering for parents, family members, and parishioners. The youth put together a PowerPoint slide presentation that shows pictures of the service they did and the people they met. Teens share stories about their experiences, about what the trip meant to them, and about how it changed their attitude about how to live. "We hold the 'reunion' several days after we return," says Walz. "And we always build in some informal visiting time for parents. They need to talk with one another about how their teens have behaved since returning. Some kids start talking and sharing stories the moment they get home, while others just want to go to bed. Some share their experiences a day or two later, and some never have much to say about the trip. At the reunion gathering, parents get a chance to compare notes with one another and find some camaraderie." Walz understands the power of the family system and how to help families adjust to changes their teens are experiencing as a result of a profound service experience.

Practical Application for Effective Youth Ministry

How do we help families adjust to the profound changes that occur in the lives of their teens? One obvious answer would be to involve the entire family in the program in which the individual participates, such as a retreat, Confirmation preparation, service experience, and so on. Some youth ministers are making innovative efforts in this area, doing such things as family catechesis and intergenerational programming.

For many aspects of youth ministry, however, it is simply not realistic for the entire family to participate. Creating *bridger experiences* to specifically connect the intensive youth experience with the individual's home and family life may be the answer in those cases. Family members can adjust to an individual's change (conversion) if they can be kept abreast of, and connected to, the ministry activities. This is the strategy Cathy Walz uses when her group serves for a week in Mexico each summer.

Recently one of our sons made his Journey retreat along with classmates from his Catholic high school. The campus ministry office orchestrated a wonderful bridger experience on the day the group returned from the retreat. All parents and family member were invited to come to the school to greet the students and reunite with them there. Prior to the students' arrival, the campus ministry team gave us parents some sound insights and advice about how our sons and daughters may have been impacted by the retreat. They gave us tips and ideas for talking about (or not talking about) the retreat with our teens.

When the bus arrived, everyone celebrated, and then some of the students shared testimonials about their experience. The session concluded with the presentation of a cross as a gift to each student. With this simple session, we parents were let "inside" the retreat, which gave us some common ground upon which to talk with our teens and to be open to whatever their responses to it might be.

I also know of one parish that developed a very effective bridger experience for young teens preparing for Confirmation. All the students are given a fifty-question review of the Catholic faith and instructed to take it home and ask anyone to help them answer the questions. The catechists are not so much concerned about correct answers as they are about spurring dialogue at home about the Catholic Christian faith. The strategy works beautifully.

A good bridger experience allows families to get a taste of the program or event, gives them information about what their loved one learned and absorbed, connects them to other families who are facing the same situation, and provides concrete ways for the family and the individual to share with each other about the intense change experience. All that helps the family system absorb the changed individual, make adjustments in the relational balance, and lend full support to the new path that the individual has chosen. When parents and families do that, they become your best partners for effective youth ministry.

Questions to Ponder

In what ways have you seen parents or families resist change, even positive change, during the adolescent years?

Of all your specific programs and activities for youth (annual retreat, Confirmation service project, and so on), which is most effective with respect to evangelization and faith formation? What makes that effort effective? What sort of change (conversion) do you often see in youth as a result of that effort?

In what ways are parents and families brought into the dynamics of that particular program or activity? Could you, or should you, do anything more to help families adjust to the change that teens experience from that program or activity?

Chapter 8

Families and Youth Faith Formation

I recall a night with my family some years ago. I had anticipated an ordinary summer evening: eating a simple dinner, taking a walk at sunset, paying some bills, catching a little television, heading off to bed on the early side—nothing special. It's not that I didn't want to be with Rene and the boys, I just didn't want or need much of anything at all. Yet there were deeper, stronger forces afoot.

I popped into the kitchen to get a clue about dinner. My son Luke, who was probably twelve years old at the time, was the only one there.

"Luke, where's Mom?"

"She's upstairs," Luke responded. "Dad, where's the olive oil?"

"In the corner cupboard, why?"

"I'm making dinner tonight!" Luke said with a sly smile. "We're having taco salad and I need to make the dressing."

Knowing that I was responsible for dishes and cleanup, and knowing Luke, I could visualize what the kitchen would look like when he finished preparing supper. So I uncharacteristically said, "Luke, do you want some help?"

His smile turned to a grin of determination. "Nope. Dad, I'm going to do this all by myself."

What could I do but begin right then to prepare myself for a long night of kitchen cleaning?

An hour later Luke called us all to the table, and we feasted on a terrific taco salad. He was filled with pride as he told us about every detail of making such a complicated meal. "It's better to use the large cheese grater than the small one. . . . You have to stir the refried beans often, or they'll stick to the pan. . . . I had to wash the lettuce three times. . . ." And on and on. Luke was so proud!

And we were proud of Luke too. The tasks of making taco salad are not so difficult, but on this particular night, our son really felt a genuine desire to serve his family. Pure heart motivated him, or perhaps it was pure grace.

During supper that evening, our older son, Nicolo, announced that he intended to lead our weekly family prayer that night. We take turns leading the family prayer, and it is the leader's job to convene the family. It is perhaps not a very good system, as our weekly prayer seldom happens every week, but it's more or less the way we've always done it.

Whenever it was Nicolo's turn, we had to remind him several times and prompt him to get going. That is why Rene and I looked at each other in surprise when he announced that he would do our family prayer that night. No prompting whatsoever. Grace.

The prayer was simple, with a Native American flavor. Using a model of the medicine wheel, Nicolo invited us to reflect on the four directions (north, south, east, west) in the context of, "What direction are you headed these days?" He offered some simple insights and then invited each of us to take a short walk in one of the four directions and offer a prayer for the Spirit's guidance. It was a simple, yet profound, experience.

God clearly graced both our boys on the very same summer evening, and I've pondered that evening ever since. The boys' behavior was certainly extraordinary, but does that mean that God's presence, grace, and behavior were equally extraordinary? I do not think so.

What was truly extraordinary was our openness and receptivity to God's grace coursing through the creases and folds of our household life that summer evening. For once the "shoulds"—the possessions, the TV schedule, the telephone, the computer games, the undone to-do list—just did not have the same magnetic pull on our consciousness. We found ourselves focused on and interested in one another. As a result, God's grace exploded in our faces. We couldn't have missed it even if we had tried.

Upon further reflection on the happenings of that summer evening, I ask why does that seem so extraordinary? Shouldn't such relational postures be more ordinary? Shouldn't we be more intentionally present to one another, allowing God's presence to unfold among us?

All children and teens have had their shining moments without any prompting. All families have been zapped with grace on occasion and have been wowed by how it all feels. God's presence is close, intimate, and constant. Imagine what your faith could be like if you made more effort to tap that presence and simply hang out with God more often. A key to family faith formation is to move from passive to active, from a posture of "stuff happens" to a posture of intentionally seeking God's activity in our lives.

Christian Practice and Discipleship

While God's grace is offered unconditionally and without price, Christians have always believed that in order for a person to fully receive grace, he or she must have personal faith. Emerging from this theology is the important notion of Christian practice. What do Christian believers do intentionally to seek and receive God's free gift of grace?

In *Practicing Our Faith: A Way of Life for a Searching People,* editor Dorothy C. Bass says it quite bluntly:

One thing about practices is that they are very down-to-earth. When people engage in a practice, they don't just talk about it, though words often play an important part. People at practice do things. . . .

. . . From one practice to another, oil is rubbed in, food is set out, water is splashed, embraces are shared. Every practice is made up of very small gestures like these. (Pp. 8–9)

One of the keys to family faith formation is intentionality. Families must choose to engage in the practices and activities that enrich their well-being and enhance their faith. These practices are both innovative and rich with tradition, and they are always life giving.

How can you put these challenges into practical language and doable activities that a believing family can grasp? In many respects, it all comes down to discipleship: As a household the family chooses to live *intentionally* as disciples of Jesus.

The next few pages contain a list of characteristics of family discipleship, and a couple practical suggestions for nurturing these characteristics within the family. If you wish, make copies of these pages and distribute them to parents.

Characteristics of Family Discipleship

Call

As a family we sense not only God's presence in our lives but also a mission and call to place ourselves at God's disposal in some way, however minor or major.

- Affirm one another's unique gifts and talents for the sake of the family and larger community.
- Be invitational without inflicting guilt. Regularly invite one another into reflection and faith action.

Commitment

We make a promise of faithfulness to God and to one another. We pledge to support one another and lift one another up when individual commitments are waning.

- Spend one-to-one time with each family member. Build personal memories together.
- Pledge your love to one another often.
- Read and tell the Old Testament stories of Yahweh's unfailing love for all people.

Values

Our decisions are rooted in core Christian values such as compassion, love, self-sacrifice, and community. When confronted with choices, big or small, we filter them through our values and try to make the best choice at the time.

- Build a strong values base by inviting discussions on provocative issues or controversial topics and allowing family members to express doubts and different opinions.
- Be willing to let other family members question you about your own views and beliefs.

Trust

We place our life in God's hands and in one another's. We don't look for a way out of the hard times; rather we look for God's guidance and support through them. We also pledge to be there for one another time and time again.

- Develop patterns of shared responsibility and interdependence. Hold each family member accountable.
- Take advantage of teachable moments. The more in touch you are with your own faith journey, the fewer teachable moments will escape you.

Practice

Like the attorney who practices law and the physician who practices medicine, as a believing family, we practice our faith. We express ourselves as believers, without apology or embarrassment, yet we never flaunt or condescend.

- Rediscover and retain the ethnic religious traditions that are your legacy.
- Read a book or two on family prayer and ritual.
- Consider both works of justice and works of mercy. In addition to caring for victims, work to change systems that victimize them.
- Integrate fun whenever possible. Combine the action with a fun event. Join with other families.

Discipline

We stay the course of our beliefs even when the "feel good" times seem to have abandoned us. God is more than a feeling or an urge to be satisfied. We seek to live our faith, even when we would prefer to do otherwise.

- Set up a regular time, like Tuesday night, for prayer. Whichever family member is in charge can lead the prayer however he or she wishes and at the end select next week's leader.
- Tell and read good stories together, including the Gospel stories.

Prayer, Ritual, and Worship

As his disciples we seek to connect with Jesus. We pray together
at home, pray for one another in our solitude, ritualize the key
moments of change in our family life, and worship regularly with
the larger community of believers.

• Give simple blessings to one another and the things you use
  daily—bikes, school supplies, and so on.
• Initiate at least one annual religious ritual in your family each
  year.
• Adopt the attitude "if it's worth doing, it's worth doing no matter
  what!" Even if you're not very good at doing ritual, it still has a
  powerful impact.

Service, Compassion, and Generosity Toward Others

We never forget that no matter how trying times may be, there are
always others who are less fortunate than us. Discipleship calls
us out of our own woes into works of mercy and justice for others.
Ironically those works often have great healing power in our own
family.

• Expose family members to advocates, victims, and situations of
  injustice. Diffuse the familiy's fear and ignorance. Ask questions
  and talk about what you don't know.
• Do "with" instead of "for." Respect and promote the dignity of
  others. Learn from those you serve.

Communion

We recognize that discipleship is not a solitary journey, so we seek
to connect with others who share our convictions. Christianity is a
communal faith. Each one of us holds pearls of grace that we must
share with all.

• Do seasonal rituals (Advent, Lent, Easter, and so on).
• Celebrate Baptism days. Light the child's baptismal candle and
  tell the story of his or her birth and Baptism.

- Try this simple exchange when leaving the house in the morning. Parent: "This is the day the Lord has made." Child: "I will rejoice and be glad."

Reflection

We take moments to look back on our day, our week, our year, and our key events to see if we can discern God's gracious activity in our lives. There is no question that God is present among us, but we must set aside time to reflect.

- Take time to listen and share. What is the talkative time of day for your child or teen?
- Use media (television, radio, Internet, and so on) and current events as discussion starters. You might start a discussion around this question: What do you think about pornography online as it relates to censorship and free speech?

Discipleship is a combination of identity and behavior. That reveals a paradox: families may consider themselves discipleship families (identity), but their behavior doesn't always reflect it. That's the rub that challenges and inspires people, in the words of John Paul II, to "become [who they] are" as a Christian family. (*Apostolic Exhortation to the Episcopate, to the Clergy, and to the Faithful of the Whole Catholic Church on the Role of the Christian Family in the Modern World [Familiaris Consortio]*, part 3, "The Role of the Christian Family," at *www.vatican.va/holy_father/john_paul_ii/apost_exhortations/documents/hf_jpii_exh_19811122_familiaris-consortio_en.html.* Accessed May 5, 2003)

Families and Christian Practice

Recent data among Christians in general and Catholics in particular show that parents and families play a crucial role in the faith formation and development of their children. Furthermore, certain activities and practices engaged in at home in a family setting are critical to the faith development of young people.

In my conversations with catechetical leaders across the country, the one consistent message I hear is this: Our traditional catechetical process of 60 to 90 minutes in age-specific classrooms once a week with a volunteer catechist is not working by itself. The research points to a partnership between the parish and the home for more positive results.

In their book *The Search for Common Ground: What Unites and Divides Catholic Americans,* James D. Davidson and his Purdue University colleagues acknowledge that family religious practice is a key predictor of a young person's adult faith practice. They report the conclusions from a rather extensive study of the beliefs and religious activity of both practicing and nonpracticing Catholics. Catholic parishioners were surveyed throughout the United States and interviewed across the state of Indiana. Generally the research highlights the importance of certain factors in establishing an adult commitment to faith. These factors point toward pastoral initiatives, such as fostering a healthy home life, early childhood experiences, and a good religious education. With respect to family and parental influence, Davidson and his colleagues summarized the research findings as follows:

> Family upbringing variables have a strong effect on the respondents' tendency, as adults, to accept traditional Catholic beliefs and practices and to agree with the Church on sexual and reproductive ethics. The strongest predictor of a high score on both of these indices is the respondent's level of childhood religiosity: respondents who report frequent Mass attendance, Communion, and prayer as children are over eight times more likely to report high levels of traditional beliefs and practices today. . . . Respondents who were close to their par-

ents or whose parents frequently talked to them about religion are twice as likely to report high levels of traditional beliefs and practices than those who were not close to their parents or whose parents "rarely" or "never" talked about religion. (Pp. 98–99)

The factor with the most impact on Catholics' religious beliefs and practices is *childhood religiosity,* which is nurtured through the family and parish or school religious education. John Roberto, noted expert on adolescent and family faith development, comments on Davidson's family upbringing study:

Family influences are extremely important, especially when parents talk about religion with their children. It seems that remaining active in one's childhood church is more attractive to those with strong family connections. Childhood religiosity affects closeness to God. The more people learn to be religious as children, the more likely they are to report experiences of the holy later in life. In other words, the way young people are raised has long-term effects on their ability to experience God in their adult years. Childhood religiosity also fosters commitment to the Church. Catholics who learn to be religious when they are young find it relatively easy to claim their Catholic identity. They also come to appreciate the benefits of being Catholic.

Davidson's family upbringing study is corroborated by a Search Institute study involving mainline Protestant denominations, which found that the three most important factors that empower the faith maturity among young people are family based. Faith maturity is a young person's ability to say yes to his or her beliefs, own them himself or herself, and act on them by his or her own choice. The research also shows that without the three key formative experiences *in the home,* genuine faith maturity is harder to come by. What are these formative experiences?

- **Family faith conversations.** Hearing their parents' faith stories is one of the most important influences on the faith of children and teenagers. Open-ended discussions on relevant and controversial issues create an atmosphere for dialogue and growth. While it is important for parents to know just where their teen stands on a given issue, it is just as important for parents to allow for a variety of opinions. It is also helpful when parents are willing to share times of doubt and questioning in their own faith journey. Sharing the rough points can create new opportunities for conversation and understanding.

- **Family ritual and devotion.** This activity moves from informal conversation to something a bit more structured and intentional. People who regularly have family devotions, prayer, or Bible reading at home tend to have higher faith maturity. Families who take some time to reflect on their daily, weekly, and seasonal habits will likely discover some opportunities for family ritual.

- **Family outreach and service.** Faced with so many problems of their own, many families are not motivated to serve others. Yet often, acts of selfless mercy can transform woes into healing as well as bring help to those in greater need. The most powerful influence on faith and family unity is working together to help others. One sure way to gain a world vision and a desire to serve others is to invite people who represent issues in the world to visit and perhaps share a meal.

God seeks a relationship with every family. Therefore, families are called to respond to God's graciousness. The free gift of God's love is always available, but when people intentionally respond to God's overtures, they find themselves in a sacramental relationship with the creator.

This relationship challenges families to an active, rather than passive, faith . . . in a family way. It requires them to be intentional about the ways they seek understanding and grow in faith . . . in a family way. It requires them to apprentice themselves to the way of life of Christian believers . . . in a family way. It challenges them to engage in practices of faith that nurture and enhance the holy relationship they have with God . . . in a family way.

Partnership Possibilities

The role of faith formation in the youth ministry program and the role of faith formation in the family have striking parallels. While the faith community of the parish faces the challenge of teaching theology, nurturing spirituality, and promoting service, the faith community of the family faces the challenge of discussing faith, sharing ritual, praying together, and engaging in service and outreach.

As parents launch their sons and daughters into young adulthood, perhaps their greatest desire is that their children take with them a personally owned and genuinely mature faith. When both the parish and the family embrace their respective challenges, those deepest desires can become reality.

The parish and the family must work in concert. For example, when the youth faith formation program teaches theology in a personal and relational manner, it only makes sense to invite teens into conversation and faith sharing with their parents and family members as part of the reflection and formation process. Likewise when families make the effort to share ritual and express a family spirituality, the parish should nurture that spirituality through liturgy, retreats, and the like. When it comes to works of mercy and acts of service, growth and learning can be phenomenal when parents and teens are working together. "Did you know that participating in service activities is a stronger predictor of a young person's faith maturity than regular participation in Sunday worship or religious education classes" (adapted from Strommen and Hardel, *Passing On the Faith*, p. 145).

While the home is not a school per se, much learning and growth occurs in the family setting. Both teens and parents learn a lot within the ordinary *and* extraordinary rhythms of daily family living. In effect, the family is a school of relationship and discipleship. The family teaches and evangelizes powerfully but informally.

Likewise the youth faith formation program simply does not operate in the manner of the home. Prescribed structure, consistent scheduling, administrative procedures, even a certain level of bureaucracy are all necessary components for your program to fulfill its mission. Amid this structure, young people receive education and form values that will serve them their entire lives.

The overarching tasks when it comes to the faith formation of teens are essentially the same for both home and school:

- discuss and teach the Catholic faith in a personal and relational manner

- nurture heartfelt spirituality through prayer, ritual, liturgy, retreats, and so on

- engage in works of mercy to help those in need and in works of justice to help change systems of oppression in society and around the world

Much good comes to teens when both the family and the parish engage in these tasks. Even greater good occurs when the parish and the family work together.

A few practical suggestions will help you facilitate that partnership. Make a point to introduce yourself and get to know parents. Make sure they know you and can remember your name. Make sure they know how to contact you. Provide sufficient information about what you cover in the faith formation program and about opportunities for parents to participate in youth ministry activities. Provide ways for parents to help with service or retreat experiences and youth liturgies.

Give parents tips, ideas, and lots of encouragement for communicating with their teens about the faith formation they are receiving. Here are a few general tips you can pass on to them. Or better yet, rephrase these tips to reflect the specific topics and issues you are covering now.

- Show genuine interest in the faith-based activities that your teen is engaged in at the parish.

- Don't ask just the who, what, where kinds of questions. Try to move beyond the facts into feelings.

- Share your own beliefs, feelings, stories, and experiences in these conversations.

- Look for ways to draw connections between the parish and your home life. Encourage your teen to be involved in the liturgical life of your parish. Volunteer yourself to be a reader, usher, or Eucharistic minister.

- Remember the power of prayer. As you pray for your teen, pray also for the parish faith community. Pray that all the teens journey through their high school years with good friends, openness to learning, and encounters of genuine spiritual growth.

Questions to Ponder

How could you build effective Christian practice in families in your regular youth ministry programming? In other words, how might you engage families in family faith conversation, family ritual and devotion, and family outreach and service?

What is one immediate and practical adjustment you could make in your youth ministry to help families grow in faith?

What is one long-term goal you could set for your youth ministry to help families grow in faith?

Chapter 9

Win the Right to Be Heard

In the early 1990s, I was working as family life director for the Archdiocese of Portland, in Oregon. I spent a great deal of time traveling up and down Interstate 5, consulting with parish leaders in our diocese on both family ministry programming and practical ways to be *family friendly* in all other parish ministries, for instance, faith formation, sacramental preparation, and Sunday worship.

One day I got a call from the director of religious education (DRE) at an average-sized parish located in suburban Salem, Oregon. She called to ask if I could meet with her staff and catechists to discuss sacramental preparation. She wanted me to address a question they had been wrestling with: How can we get parents more interested in understanding the sacraments of Baptism, the Eucharist, Reconciliation (also called Penance), and Confirmation? She explained that when parents came to the designated parent sessions (two sessions required for each sacrament), they seemed to "glaze over" as soon as the catechist started talking about the meaning of the sacrament. Two things were clear: (1) Parents genuinely cared about the faith formation of their children and teens, and (2) the catechetical staff was well versed in the theological and pastoral underpinnings of these sacraments. Yet it was obvious the Good News of these sacraments wasn't hitting home. "How do we get those parents more engaged when they come to those mandatory sessions?" asked the DRE.

I tried to refer this DRE to our diocesan catechetical consultant who surely knew a lot more about sacrament preparation than I did. But the DRE insisted this was a "parent problem" and that it was more appropriate for me to help her and her staff. I agreed to meet, though I didn't have a clue how I might help them. A few days later, the DRE, her assistant, the parish youth minister (paid staff member), a handful of volunteers connected to each of the sacraments, and I gathered in a meeting room and set to work. They reiterated the problem for me, and we brainstormed possible solutions. We prioritized our ideas. We discounted most of them. We took a break. We were circling the airport looking for the runway.

Near the end of our full morning together, someone said something quite simple and yet deeply profound: "All morning we've been looking at the problem from the viewpoint of teaching about the sacraments. What if we looked at the problem from the viewpoint of *what parents need?*" Ah ha! Suddenly we were approaching the problem from a completely different perspective, and the ideas started flowing. We asked ourselves what key questions might be on the minds of parents when they walk into the parish hall for their sacramental prep night, and then we asked ourselves how we might build toward the sacrament from there.

In a matter of just a few minutes, we established a hierarchy of four questions that the sessions for each sacrament could be designed to answer. We all agreed on the first one rather quickly because we felt that it was a question always playing on the internal Walkman of all parents: *Is my child normal?* (Is my child's behavior disturbed or just disturbing?) To address this question, we decided to create a simple discussion process for parents to reflect on the basic developmental needs of children in the specific age-group using small amounts of content and a lot of small-group conversation.

The second question stemmed from the first: *How can I be a better parent for my child?* The group decided to provide the parents with a handout containing a number of parenting tips for children in the specific age-group and invite them into more small-group conversation. That would fill the room with conversation, interaction, and energy.

The third question the group came up with was *What does faith have to do with my child, our family, and my efforts to be a better parent?* The group decided to develop some tips, ideas, and suggestions on— you guessed it—three key activities: family faith conversation, family ritual and devotion, and family outreach and service. They then decided to gather the parents again for more conversation.

Finally, the fourth question, the one the parents have been waiting for: *How does this sacrament fit into the context of our family and our efforts to grow in faith?* In response, the group decided that the catechist would give the lesson on the pastoral and theological understanding of the sacrament. There would be less time to cover all the material using this four-question strategy, but the group anticipated that parents would be ready to hear it and receive it. After implementing this strategy, the group realized they had been right on target. In fact, many parents had questions, anecdotes, and additional insights to add to the lesson.

Parents' Agenda

The moral of the previous story is simple: Before parents will be able to embrace your agenda they must know that you understand theirs. As a youth minister, you can become so preoccupied with the faith content of your work that you leave the realities of family living behind. The fact that the *latest thinking* on the theology and pastoral application of the sacrament of Confirmation is *not* at the forefront of the minds of parents of teenagers does not reflect poor faith priorities on their part. On any given Tuesday night, when parents walk into the parish hall for just such a meeting, it is normal and natural that any number of other home concerns will occupy, front and center, their psyche.

A May 2002 study conducted by the YMCA and Search Institute reveals some key findings on what occupies parents' agendas these days:

- A majority of parents surveyed are "going it alone" in raising children and teenagers. Fifty-three percent indicated that they do not regularly ask for parenting help, advice, or support from immediate or extended family, friends, or community resources. Only 4 percent indicate that they receive support from all three of these sources. Those who do seek support are most likely to turn to family and friends. Only 11 percent turn to community resources for help, advice, and support. [If we wait for parents to come to us, it is not likely to happen. As a faith community, we must reach out to them.]

- A key but often lacking resource for parents is a strong relationship with their spouse or partner. The parents interviewed (both married and unmarried) who experience an excellent partner relationship are more likely to feel successful and up to the challenge of parenting. They are more likely to do things that help their kids grow up strong and healthy, to feel successful and confident as parents, to experience fewer challenges as parents, and to be open to outside support and learning. Unfortunately only half the parents interviewed claimed a strong relationship with their partner. [What would it say to the youth in your program if you made a concerted effort to strengthen the marriage of their parents through such things as evenings of enrichment, sending home articles and reflections, and so on?]

- Most parents face ongoing challenges. Struggles related to job, finances, overstuffed calendar, marriage, and conflicts among children are rampant and commonplace. What used to be the occasional family who experienced an acute stressor has increased to the point where most families are dealing with some sort of serious anxiety at any given moment. As a result, parents feel unprepared for situations that arise, overwhelmed by all that is happening, and generally unsupported by family and friends. These factors contribute to their feeling dissatisfied with their parenting.

- The things parents say would really help them are not difficult to provide. They seek *affirmation* for doing a good job as parents. Nearly 70 percent said this would help them. Over 70 percent said they would benefit from having other adults whom they trust spend time with their kids. [My experience with intergenerational programs indicates that both of these needs can be met when you bring parents and teens together.]

- Most parents generally feel successful as parents most of the time. They do many things to help their children grow up healthy and strong: showing love and support (97 percent); teaching basic values such as equality, honesty, and responsibility (89 percent); and helping their children feel good at something (87 percent). [This point shows us how resilient parents are to the pressures and challenges they face, and how resolved they are to raising healthy kids.]

(Adapted from "Building Strong Families Fact Sheet"; bracketed material added)

Notice that faith concerns are not listed among parental concerns. On your more cynical days of ministry, you may be tempted to conclude that parents do not really care about the faith formation of their children and teens, at least not to the extent that they care about their kids' social and athletic formation. My point, however, which my experience confirms, is that when you show parents that you understand and sympathize with all the pressures and challenges they face and that you want to help and support them in concrete ways they will more readily respond to the faith message you have for them and their teens.

Parent Intimidation

In the spring of 2002, I was asked to facilitate a retreat for a group of youth ministers from the Pacific Northwest. During one of the sessions, the discussion centered on parents and how to relate to them. Among the twenty of us gathered, over half were young adults—single, unattached, non-parents—who had recently launched into the world themselves. They were bright, dedicated, creative, . . . and young.

One of those young adults, a very bright, clearly competent young woman, spoke up and admitted what a number of the others were holding in their minds and hearts: "While I feel perfectly comfortable with kids, whenever I have to interact with their parents, I feel intimidated and tongue-tied. I become very much aware of my own youth and inexperience. While I know a lot about teenagers, I don't know anything about parenting. How do I connect with them? I feel especially inadequate whenever I need to call a parent to discuss a problem that the teen has or if the teen has been disruptive or misbehaving. If the parent challenges me at all, I feel utterly defenseless." There were a few nods around the room. I understood completely, because that is exactly how I felt when I was a young adult parish youth minister. I wondered if she was expressing a feeling that the other young adults were experiencing.

As a parent of teens, my heart went out to that young woman. I admired her for simply admitting how she felt. Several parents and veteran youth ministers were in the room, so she took a risk in expressing her feelings. No one else in the group admitted to the same feelings, but clearly there were others in the same situation. Instead the group chimed in with ideas and suggestions to help her solve her problem. Again I admired her for staying in the hot seat, while she and the others benefited from the brainstorming.

The group generated several good ideas:

- Be honest with parents about your youth and lack of experience in parenting, but remain confident in your understanding of teens and your ability to relate to them in other settings.

- Use "partnership" language with parents. Let them know that you are trying to work with them in the faith formation of their teens.

- Ask parents questions about their teens. Ask how the young person behaves at home, and compare that to his or her behavior in the parish or youth-group setting. If the teen is exhibiting a problem behavior, be very clear and descriptive about that behavior. Avoid labeling and interpreting, allowing the parent to come to his or her own conclusion. Close the conversation by asking, "How do you think we can work together to resolve this difficulty?"

- Build relationships with as many parents as you can. Introduce yourself personally whenever appropriate. Reach out to parents and make contact in the same ways you attempt to do so with kids. Set a goal to have at least one personal interaction with every parent.

- Find something personal and positive to say to each parent about his or her teen. That puts goodwill in the bank if the time comes when you have to call that parent about a problem.

- When working with parent volunteers, exercise the authority you are entrusted with as the one responsible for the youth ministry program. Remember, you know how to do your job, otherwise you would not have been hired. Part of your job involves managing volunteers, some of whom will be parents of teens and who may have strong opinions on how things should go. Without being abusive or dictatorial, exercise your leadership when and where it is needed. If your core group of leaders operates on a consensus model of decision making, you still need to effectively facilitate the decision-making process. You will gain the confidence of all your volunteers, including those who are parents.

Like many discussions of this nature, this one ended without the group landing on a hard and fast answer for every situation. Yet I am confident that every one of us took away at least one small pearl of wisdom.

Practical Application for Effective Youth Ministry

How do you win the right to be heard? In addition to following the relational tips listed in the previous section, three effective strategies can help you be heard.

First, offer lots of ideas, tips, and suggestions for helping families smooth out their rough spots and function together on a day-to-day basis. Consider these five key moments for daily family living. Provide a constant stream of ways parents can intentionalize the following moments:

- exits and entries (leaving in the morning and returning in the evening)

- car time

- mealtime

- bedtime

- memory-making time

Think of those as the moments when ordinary family living can intermingle with spiritual matters for the family. Use the parish bulletin, the youth ministry newsletter, and any other communication channels to share those ideas with parents of teens. Whenever you gather parents, ask them for their ideas and experiences for intentionalizing those moments. Ask if you can share those ideas with other parents.

Second, balance "gathered" and "nongathered" program time. Take a look at the scope of your youth ministry programming over the course of a year. What percentage of that programming involves parent-teen interaction outside the parish hall or aside from gathered events? In other words, what amount of your programming is dedicated to "home" work—teens and their parents engaged in conversation or ritual or service in the comfort of their home and family life? If your percentage is 0, what might you do to bump it up to 5? If your percentage is 10, you're doing great, but what might you do bump it to 15 for the coming year? A good way to begin with nongathered programming is with homework itself. At a gathered faith formation session, give the young people a homework assignment that involves talking with family members or interviewing their parents about the topic of the session. Ask the teens to report the results at the next gathering.

Third, balance age-segmented classes with intergenerational events. Magic happens occasionally when parents and teens are gathered in the context of faith formation. They engage in conversations that they would not ordinarily have at home, and those conversations can be a catalyst for further faith exploration. Intergenerational gatherings can and should become integral to effective youth faith formation. As I write this book, several of my editorial colleagues at Saint Mary's Press are preparing a new parish high school youth ministry curriculum that we called the Total Faith series. Among its many innovative components is an intergenerational session for each of the core topics of the program. If you use Total Faith, you are expected to gather teens, parents, grandparents, and others on a regular basis.

Questions to Ponder

When it comes to interacting with parents of teens, what intimidates you the most? What makes you feel inadequate? What makes you feel confident and capable?

Think about your experience in youth ministry, whether you've been doing it for many years or just a few months. Recall a positive encounter with a parent or group of parents. What made it positive? What did you do to "win the right to be heard"? How might you have blown it?

Had you been assigned to write this chapter, what advice would you give to your fellow youth ministry colleagues on winning the right to be heard with parents?

Chapter 10

When There Is a Problem

Generally this book presumes that parents and families sincerely desire faith growth and spiritual development for their teens. It's a safe presumption. Yet if you have been involved in youth ministry for more than just a couple months, you have likely encountered some parents and families who, for a variety of reasons, do not seem to put much effort into helping their teens along in faith growth and spiritual development. What gives?

As outlined in the previous chapters, you seek to develop relationships with parents in order to partner with them for effective faith formation of teens. But what should you do when it's not possible to develop that relationship? What about those parents who are in serious conflict with their teens? What about those parents who are in conflict with the Church? What about those parents who are in serious conflict with each other? What about those parents who are upset with you or with the way you run your youth ministry program? What can you do when you know that family issues and problems are an obstacle to a teen's developing faith formation?

A True Story

The following story, first printed in the book *Growing Up Girl: Sharing Your Heart with Your Mom* (Winona, MN: Saint Mary's Press, 2003), by Eileen Pettycrew, is a true story shared by a woman named Patricia, who was raised in New York. Her story not only reflects the extreme of family issues and problems but also serves to show that many families cope with serious problems, and many teens of those families put on a smile each day to prevent the rest of us from seeing the difficult reality in which they live at home.

When I was twelve my parents put my sixteen-year-old brother in charge of caring for my other brother and me while our parents worked. From the start the arrangement was barely tolerable. My oldest brother insisted that I ask permission to read a book, eat a snack, or even go to the bathroom. He carved out a niche for himself as a dictator who controlled my every move.

Soon my life spiraled out of control. My brother began to sexually abuse me. He chased me around the house, cornered me, and forced me to do unimaginable things. Day after nightmarish day he came after me. If I didn't comply with his demands, he made my life even more miserable.

One day I spent hours hiding from my brother. I managed to stay just out of his reach, a tactic that enraged him. When my father got home from work, my brother launched into a tirade, telling Father how I had refused to obey him. He made it sound like I was an uncooperative brat. Of course my brother didn't tell my father that it was his sexual advances that I had refused. Nor did I.

A tornado blew through my head. My brother was the one in the wrong, not me. Fury burned in me like red-hot coals, but I didn't have time to let my anger rise to the surface. Watching my father closely, I could see he had arrived home already agitated and in a volatile mood. Without warning he grabbed me and began to strike me with the strap. As I endured the cruel punishment, I could see my brother smirking at me. I longed to tell Father the truth about my brother. That would wipe that smirk off his face once and for all.

In Father's holster, only inches away from my face when I was being beaten, was Father's gun. It was the gun he carried for his job as a bridge and tunnel officer. As soon as I saw the gun I knew I was doomed to suffer again and again at the hands of my brother. I realized I would never be able to tell Father the truth about what my brother was doing to me. If I did I was sure Father would whip out that gun and shoot my brother. I didn't want to have that on my conscience.

Telling my mother what was going on was out of the question as well. She was overwhelmed with her full-time job, with paying the bills, and with trying to keep our home running, even at a barely functional level. I thought that if I told her she might have an emotional breakdown and be sent away. Where would that leave me? I would be left at home with my abusive brother and my unpredictable father. No, I couldn't tell my mother.

I was also afraid to tell my schoolteacher what was happening at home. I did not want to be responsible for my father's actions if he should find out what my brother was doing to me. I struggled to concentrate on multiplication, long division, fractions, reading, government, and history. None of these things held any relevance for me. Afraid to reveal my secret, I was caught in a hideous trap with no way to escape.

When I entered eighth grade I realized I could create my own sphere of happiness away from my brother and father. Although my life at home was unbearable, life at school didn't have to be. So I started to smile at my classmates, friends, and teachers. At first I had to force myself to do it. Many times I felt as parched and cracked as a sunbaked desert. I thought if I kept smiling, my face might break into a million pieces. Still I smiled even when I didn't feel like it.

After a while my face changed. My muscles seemed less rigid. My mouth began to naturally turn up at the corners. I felt a light shine through my eyes, a light that poured forth from my heart. I smiled so much that my English teacher, a severe and stern nun, called me Miss Sunshine. I loved my honorary title and wore it proudly, trying to smile whenever I could.

My smiling changed nothing at home though. The abuse continued until I got the courage to move out at age sixteen. Once gone from the house, I confided in a trustworthy person who was willing to help me reveal my secret. With my friend's encouragement, I gained the confidence to confront my brother. I told my brother that if he continued to abuse me, my friend would tell our parents or go to the authorities. After that conversation my brother stopped abusing me. Until that time I had done what I could to make my life bearable.

While this story may seem extreme, unfortunately it is not extraordinary. Many children and teens experience some form of abuse before leaving home as young adults. This reality is undoubtedly true for some young people you serve. You may or may not be aware of their experience. Carrying a secret burden, those young people may find it difficult, if not impossible, to "hear," let alone embrace, the Good News of Jesus Christ.

Other families, though not abusive, might find themselves struggling mightily with the changes that adolescence brings. Family relationships become strained, conflict rears its ugly head, and individuals say and do hurtful things to one another. Teens act out with risky behavior, experimenting with alcohol, drugs, sex, and the like. Parents feel embarrassed and, consequently, do all they can to cover up the struggles. Again, the message of the Gospel seems impractical and irrelevant.

Symptoms

When a family is stressed, the usual balance of relationships and inter-action is disturbed, and a symptom occurs. It is easy to mistake the symptom for the problem, but in reality the symptom reflects a source of tension infecting the entire family. Furthermore, the symptom will likely show itself in the most vulnerable person in the family system, not necessarily in the person or relationship responsible for the stress.

The most vulnerable person in a family is the one least capable of dealing with the stress. Years ago, when my children were quite young, my wife and I moved our family from Spokane, Washington, to Portland, Oregon. Contrary to the U-Haul advertising slogan "Moving Is an Adventure," the move was a stressor, to say the least. Once we settled into our new home, we took a vacation to the coast. Luke, our then four-year-old, had never seen the ocean, and we were anticipating him frolicking in the sand and surf for four days. Not. He was grumpy, whiny, and upset the entire time. In fact, his inconsolable behavior lasted for several weeks, to the point where we were beginning to worry about his emotional balance. But as the anxiety of our move lessened, and as we were able to give better attention to our children, Luke became a happier child. He was the symptom bearer of the family stress over moving to a new city.

In your relational ministry with teens and their families who are struggling, if you focus only on the symptom bearer, you will likely miss the problem altogether. The symptom bearer often "screams" for attention, to be the center of focus, but most often that person is not responsible for the problem. That is especially true for teens whose identity and belonging needs are peaking. Combine those needs with a family stress that struggling teens are ill-equipped to handle, simply because of their youth, and you end up with a classic symptom bearer who becomes the acceptable scapegoat for the family problem. After all, teenagers are supposed to have problems, right?

Adolescents may act out with bizarre, even destructive behavior, seeking attention from their parents. They may be crying out for love and even boundaries because Mom and Dad are too preoccupied with their own issues. Teens may make themselves the center of attention to distract parents from marital problems, thus keeping the family intact.

Tunnel vision focused solely on either the symptom or the one exhibiting the symptom will yield the least helpful results. However, not every adolescent misbehavior is rooted in serious family dysfunction. Nearly all teens make poor choices at one time or another. A fifteen-year-old boy mentioned to me that the counselors at his Catholic high school were always trying to diagnose some type of problem in the family whenever the slightest thing went wrong.

In your relational work with teens and their families, you must keep in mind their individual developmental issues, but you must also avoid tunnel vision that fails to see family connections and significant relationships. You might find it helpful to reflect on the problem situation with the following questions:

- How well do I know this young person and his or her feelings, habits, and attitudes?

- Is the problem a result of relatively normal adolescent struggles, or is it cause for greater concern?

- What do I know about this young person's family, and how does that knowledge help me interpret his or her story?

- Has this young person displayed a change in behavior or attitude recently? Has anything significant happened in recent weeks or months?

Adolescent family relationships are complex and vulnerable. You must be cautious and neutral in your efforts to intervene. When encountering teens who have apparent problems, follow these guidelines:

- Reserve judgment about the rightness or wrongness of the behavior. Placing blame on the teen or any family member has no benefit for resolution and change.

- Talk with the teen about the significant relationships in his or her life, especially relationships with family members. It is likely that at least one family member contributes to the distress.

- Get to know family members. Who is the vulnerable one in the system? Do you see other symptoms of trouble?

- Know the referral agencies available for help. Don't be afraid to recommend them. Many struggling families know they need help, but they don't know how to take the first step.

- Do not try to be a family therapist. Leave that to the experts.

Triangles

In relationships, when tensions build and disagreements emerge, as they surely will, individuals are tempted to bring in a third party to diffuse the anxiety or to have someone on their side. A triangle prevents direct communication between two parties in conflict. In most cases that prevents the two parties from resolving their issue. In other cases a triangle is purposely established, perhaps with an intermediary, because that may be the only way to solve the problem.

Triangles are basic to human relationships. Two people cannot maintain unresolved conflict or sustained intimacy without bringing in a third party. Focusing on the third party deflects emotional intensity. Out of a genuine desire to help, heal, and reconcile, you may find yourself frequently hooked into triangles, most of which are not helpful in the long run. Perhaps the most difficult pastoral approach is to let two people manage their own relationship. You might have a difficult time resisting an invitation to join in as a third party when a parent confronts you with a comment like, "If the youth program accomplished what it's supposed to, my son wouldn't be so disrespectful at home." Or, "If the youth group spent more time studying the Bible and traditional Catholic prayers, we wouldn't have a family argument every Sunday morning about going to Mass." If a parent directed comments like those at you, you would likely want to respond. Yet a moment of pause might reveal that those statements are emotionally laden with other family issues completely out of your control.

You can, however, be helpful in sensitive circumstances without getting hooked into triangles. Consider these strategies:

- Stay calm. Try to take a low-key approach when someone confronts you with conflict and stress. Avoid fueling the driving force with more anxiety and intensity.
- Stay out. Resist the temptation to resolve their issues. Your advice, analyzing, and lecturing is heeded only enough to keep you entangled in the web. The real solution lies in their managing their own relationship.
- Hang in. Maintain emotional closeness with both parties, communicating your care, concern, and confidence that whatever the problem may be, the two of them can work it out.
  (Adapted from Harriet Lerner, *The Dance of Anger,* p. 183)

Triangles tend to repeat themselves when new struggles emerge. Take note of family members and whose side they choose when tensions arise. Also keep in mind that triangles do not always include three *people.* Sometimes the third party is a job, an emotional memory, a chronic illness, a substance dependency, and so on.

Also take into account the principle of nonanxious presence. Your pastoral presence to a teen and his or her family who may be struggling can be either an anxiety booster or an anxiety breaker. The level of anxiety in any system of human relationships provides the key for effective functioning. If each member of a family is walking on eggshells, waiting for one more minor stressor that may push them all beyond the breaking point, the family's ability to function in a healthy manner is severely limited.

Anxiety infuses any system with higher voltage. Your *anxious* presence in the significant life-issue situations of teens and their families will have a consistently negative impact, in spite of good intentions. Your *nonanxious* presence, however, will act as a circuit breaker, diffusing the high voltage already present.

Implications for Youth Ministry

Getting pulled into relational triangles with teens and their parents is an occupational hazard for youth workers. The more you seek to build relationships, and the more you genuinely care about young people's lives, the easier it may be to get drawn in. Be aware of your own personal need to be needed.

Recognize the difference between getting hooked into a triangle and effective *intervention*. Because of your consistent relational work with teens and their families, you will likely encounter situations that, for the safety and well-being of those present, warrant intervention. To avoid triangulation, remain neutral with all parties (don't take sides), employ the efforts of nonanxious presence (stay calm, stay out, hang in), and keep referral information on hand (phone number of a counselor, therapist, or professional helper). Remember that the conflict likely goes deeper than the immediate struggle; remain calmly focused on honest communication and the value of relationships.

Families are mysterious and unpredictable. They are living, growing, and changing. New wrinkles emerge every day. Mitch Finley, noted author on family life, put it this way:

Family living is a comfort, God knows, and family living is a grand and glorious pain. Almost every day you'd as soon hop a slow boat to China as stick around. Almost every day you'd give your very life for those ne'er do-wells you live with. Almost every day you do. God knows.

Questions to Ponder

Recall an encounter when you were an effective nonanxious presence, helping others resolve the problem. Replay the experience in your mind. What specific things did you do or say that helped to diffuse the anxiety?

Recall an encounter when you were not so effective in helping others resolve a problem. Replay that experience in your mind. Why do you think you were not effective?

Do you have referral sources on hand for such services as family counseling, emergency shelter, abuse prevention, and so on? Do you know those practitioners personally? Can you feel confident recommending them to a troubled family?

A Christian Vision for Family Life

The Church holds a rich vision for marriage and family living. Though the focus of this book is on parents and partnering with parents for the sake of the faith formation of teens, everything in this book is rooted in a Christian vision for family life. In this appendix I simply make explicit what I imply throughout the chapters of this book. Putting words and labels to those implications gives them life and meaning.

I invite you to read this appendix at least twice. Read it the first time in the context of your role in ministry with teens, for that fits the overall focus of this book. What about this book confirms and or challenges you in your ministry with teens? Read this appendix a second time in the context of your personal family living—either the family in which you grew up or the family you have created as an adult. What confirms, challenges, and invites you and your family to grow in faith?

A Bit o' Theology

The Christian family is holy and sacred. This is a simple but profound statement that carries far-reaching implications for the Church and all believers. Interestingly most believers would not hesitate to affirm the truth of that statement. Something about living in a family, even amidst its foibles and quirks and problems and dysfunction, reveals a sort of wholesome sacredness. Most of the time we cannot explain it, but we know it is there.

Holy and sacred does not mean problem-free—not by any means. It does not even necessarily mean "capable of solving our problems." All it means is that we are believers and that we have occasionally encountered the Mystery of love.

The family is holy and sacred not by pure happenstance. The family must ascend to belief and faith, intentionally pursuing God's presence, which lingers among the ordinary and extraordinary events of family life. However weak and imperfect, intentionality is key.

It is one thing for families themselves to acknowledge the sacredness of family life and quite another matter for the Church to theologically say so, but that is just what the Church has done—many times. Perhaps compared to other proclamations by the Church, that one does not get much press, but that does not make it any less true. Unfortunately this small but significant theological point often gets overlooked by theologians in their writings today.

Yet it cannot be denied that "the earliest Christians were converts from Judaism, and the center of Jewish religious life (particularly after the destruction of the Temple in A.D. 70) was the home, not the synagogue. So it makes sense that the early Jewish Christians would hold family life in the highest esteem" (Mitch Finley, "Family Orphaned by the Church"). The Acts of the Apostles and the letters of Saint Paul reflect positive attitudes toward family life that must have been so common as to have simply been taken for granted.

In Mitch and Kathy Finley's book *Building Christian Families*, they point out that "[in] the late fourth century, St. John Chrysostom—in his sermons on the Book of Genesis and in his commentary on the Epistle to the Ephesians—described the family as *ekklesia*, the Greek Second Testament term for church. Only once did John

Chrysostom use the diminutive form *ekklesiola,* 'little church'; more often simply called the family *ekklesia*—church" (pp. 14–15). Chrysostom knew the family household had all the necessary ingredients to reflect and resemble the Christian community.

Pope Leo XIII declared that "the family was ordained of God . . . It was before the church, or rather the first form of the church on earth" (p. 15). More recently, in his book *Sacraments and Sacramentality,* theologian Bernard Cooke says, "The Christian family is meant to be the most basic instance of Christian community, people bonded together by their shared relationship to the risen Jesus" (p. 92).

Popes Paul VI and John Paul II have also affirmed the sacred nature of the Christian family. In *Evangelii Nuntiandi,* his apostolic exhortation on evangelization, Pope Paul VI said, "There should be found in every Christian family the various aspects of the entire Church."

In his exhortation on the family, *Familiaris Consortio,* Pope John Paul II states, "Among the fundamental tasks of the Christian family is its ecclesial task: the family is placed at the service of building up the kingdom of God in history by participating in the life and mission of the Church." The Holy Father goes on to say that "the Christian family also builds up the Kingdom of God in history through the everyday realities that concern and distinguish its state of life." In developing this theme, Pope John Paul II, drawing on the teaching of Vatican Council II and Pope Paul VI, stresses that the specific conjugal love of spouses, the love meant to be expressed in their lives and extended through their family and children to the community in which they live is what "constitutes the nucleus of the saving mission of the Christian family in the Church and for the Church."

In their 1994 pastoral message to families, *Follow the Way of Love,* the U.S. Catholic bishops state quite profoundly the Church's teaching on family:

A family is our first community and most basic way in which the Lord gathers us, forms us and acts in the world. The early Church expressed this truth by calling the Christian family a *domestic church* or *church of the home.*

This marvelous teaching was under-emphasized for centuries, but reintroduced by the Second Vatican Council. Today we are still uncovering its rich treasure.

The point of the teaching is simple, yet profound. As Christian families, you not only belong to the Church, but your daily life is a true expression of the Church.

Your domestic church is not complete by itself, of course. It should be united with and supported by parishes and other communities within the larger Church. Christ has called you and joined you to himself in and through the sacraments. Therefore, you share in one and the same mission that he gives to the whole Church.

Notice what the bishops did *not* say. They did not say that when Christian families say their meal prayers, when they gather around the Advent wreath, when they worship at Mass, they are a true expression of Church. Of course all these are true expressions, but the bishops use the term *daily life.* Believing families seeking God's presence in their normal activities, in their *daily life* as a family, is a true expression of the Church.

As ministry leaders you must give serious thought and reflection to the bishops' statement, "As Christian families, you not only belong to the Church, but your daily life is a true expression of the Church" *(Follow the Way of Love).* What if you truly believed this? What would your programs and ministries look like?

Keep in mind that this theology is prescriptive and visionary, as opposed to descriptive and analytical. These teachings recognize the redemptive power of a God who loves so fully and unconditionally that holiness and sacredness are unconditionally available.

As Mitch and Kathleen Finley say: "*Family Spirituality* means no more and no less than this: A family's ongoing attempts to live every dimension of its life in communion with the Cross and Resurrection of Jesus the Christ" *(Building Christian Families,* p. 18). They also recognize the important relationship between the church of the home and the church of the parish:

> The local parish and the universal church depend upon families for their fundamental vitality as they strive to make Christ present in the modern world. It also means that as families go, so goes the church. If we want a strong church in the future, we must pay attention to family life in the church today. (P. 16)

The Christian vision of family life speaks about the family as a community of life and love. It proclaims that family life is sacred and that family activities are holy, that God's love is revealed and communicated in new ways each and every day through Christian families. This Christian vision of family life calls families to a unique identity and mission. The Christian family *is* holy and sacred. As a result, families can come to believe that God dwells among them, and so they respond to God's gracious activity in their lives.

A Particular Spirituality

As we recognize the holy and sacred nature of family life, we encounter a spirituality that relishes in the immanence of God's presence and love. This is quite different from God's transcendent love.

Most of us Catholic Christians have a better understanding of God's transcendent love, referring to the idea that God is so great, so awesome, so magnificent, that God is literally "out of this world." That is just what *transcendent* means. God far exceeds any human effort to fully understand God. Knowing we cannot fully embrace all that is God, how do we go about trying to do so in our spiritual journey? If the God we seek transcends our immediate world, would it not make sense for us to also try to transcend our immediate world? This is a core notion of monastic spirituality: If we remove ourselves from the noise, clutter, and distractions of life, we can more easily and more richly connect with the transcendent God.

This is why we seek solitude, quiet, and peace when we pray. This is why we go on retreat. We find God's transcendent love when we empty our minds and hearts of all the noise and distractions of life. When we spend time in quiet prayer and meditation, we ground ourselves with the real but unseen God, and we are then empowered to carry on with the pressures of our day.

God's immanent love is not exactly the opposite of transcendence but is a contrasting complement. While God is literally out of this world, at the same time God is also as close as the air we breathe. The breadth and depth of God's love is so great we can find it within the noise, clutter, and sometimes chaos of our lives.

God's immanent love opens up the possibility of a spirituality that complements the monastic style of solitude, meditation, and contemplation. It is a spirituality of movement and noise. It is the art of discovering the Spirit within those very things that we might consider distractions.

Ideally our spirituality includes our pursuing both the immanence and transcendence of God's love. One is not better than the other; rather each shares some dependence on the other. I, personally, take great comfort in this distinction. Why? Because my lifestyle does not lend itself to frequent and prolonged periods of solitude and prayerful meditation. Sitting down to pray in a corner of my house somehow sends a signal to all family members that now is the exact time they need to ask Dad a question, or dust that very corner, or vacuum that room. So, while my efforts to transcend to God's love are often thwarted, I am grateful for God's presence in the here and now.

Yet, of course, pursuing God's transcendent love is not just for the monks, mystics, and monastics. Everyone needs regular periods of quiet and solitude amid the frenetic pace of life. If I don't take a few minutes for quiet centering each morning, I don't make it to the end of the day. I lose my ability to be present to others, even to myself, long before I am allowed to seek my bed again. The essence of spirituality is presence. If I can't be present to myself or others, I certainly cannot tune in to the presence of the Spirit.

While centuries of development have gone into monastic spirituality, far less systematic development has been dedicated to a spirituality of immanence. Therefore, folks like you and me must take the risk of sharing with one another our simple encounters with God, hopefully enriching and enlivening this spirituality.

God's immanent love is rooted in the very nature of married and household life. Instead of trying to adapt a monastic-style spirituality to the hectic lives we lead (as spouses, parents, professionals, and so on), we seek to develop a spirituality that emerges from the very essence of our lives in the world.

In her book *Experiencing God with Your Children,* Kathy Coffey offers several lovely insights to further explore a spirituality of immanence and the sacred nature of family living. These passages are worth noting:

> How providential that God should have infinite variety! For all the different seasons in children's growing up, a different face of God can turn to their deepest longings and respond to their deepest desires. . . . We can explore the nature of God throughout a lifetime and never reach the end. . . . (P. 13)
>
> . . . Our first, most precious learnings about God can come only at home. If, in that small sphere, we do not fall in love with God, it would be pointless to continue our quest. . . .
>
> Parents and children who do meet God at home are more inclined to broaden their orbit and find God everywhere. . . .
>
> Using home as the starting point and the end of our theology should not seem so odd. For Jesus, earthly life began in the small circle of affection at Bethlehem, and ended in the circle of his mother's arms. . . . (P. 14)

Perhaps it is like [a serendipitous scene] when parents and children enter into a joint exploration of God. How can we *not* go? No matter what other agendas concern us, no matter what wisdom we want to give our children, the divine person is uniquely compelling, drawing us with an infinite love. The search for God becomes a quest for creator, lover, parent, friend, our reason for being, the meaning of our lives, the beauty, the fulfillment of our days. . . . (P. 16)

A friend who is completing his doctorate in theology tells how he agonized over a talk he would give at church on some point about God that was elusive. When his three-year-old daughter asked what was troubling him, he explained as best he could that he'd thought hard about God but still wasn't fully understanding God. She reassured him with a touch on his shirt, "Don't worry, Dad. God is right there in your pocket." All our struggles to nuance and refine can sputter into silence before a child's clarity. (P. 24)

When families recognize their own holy and sacred nature, they also find it easier to see and experience God in the bigger world around them. God's presence permeates all reality. Family living can provide the foundation and formation that empowers children and teens to be on the lookout for God's presence as they launch into the big wide world.

Conclusion

Family life is the first and most formative experience of acceptance and belonging along life's journey. It is our first experience of community. When the family connects with the community of the church, the family becomes the church of the home. In a homily in Perth, Australia, in 1986, Pope John Paul II made the following statement:

The family is the domestic church. The meaning of this traditional Christian idea is that the home is the Church in miniature. The

Church is the sacrament of God's love. She is a communion of faith and love. She is a mother and teacher. She is at the service of the whole human family as it goes forward towards its ultimate destiny. In the same way the family is a community of life and love. It educates and leads its members to their full human maturity and it serves the good of all along the road of life. In its own way it is a living image and historical representation of the mystery of the Church. The future of the world and of the Church pass way of the family.

This papal teaching reinforces the challenge to recognize the family as an authentic expression of the church of the home. All parish ministries and programs must recognize the unique ministry of the family and must search for ways to partner with families.

Rev. Tom Boland, the first president of the National Association of Catholic Family Life Ministers, offers apt words to close this appendix:

As the basic community of believers, bound in love to one another, the family is the arena in which the drama of redemption is played out. The dying and rising with Christ is most clearly manifested. Here, the cycle of sin, hurt, reconciliation, and healing is lived out over and over again. In family life is found the church of the home: where each day "two or three are gathered" in the Lord's name; where the hungry are fed; where the thirsty are given drink; where the sick are comforted. It is in the family that the Lord's injunction to forgive "seventy times seven" is lived out in the daily reconciliation of husband, wife, parent, child, grandparent, brothers, sisters, extended kin. (Unpublished personal note)

Appendix B

Helpful Resources

Benson, Peter, et al. *What Kids Need to Succeed: Proven Practical Ways to Raise Good Kids.* Minneapolis: Free Spirit Publishing, 1998. 800-735-7323, *www.freespirit.com.* Kids who succeed have specific developmental assets in their lives, including family support, self-esteem, and hope. The more assets young people have, the less likely they are to use alcohol and other drugs, have sex too soon, and engage in other problematic behaviors. Based on a groundbreaking nationwide study, this book spells out forty assets—good things every young person needs.

Brennan, Tina. *Sacred Gifts: Extraordinary Lessons from My Ordinary Teens.* Winona, MN: Saint Mary's Press, 2003. 800-533-8095, *www.smp.org.* Middle teens, just by living their ever eventful lives, shape and enrich the adults around them. *Sacred Gifts* taps the opportunities for growth and sacred insight that come when parents ponder and appreciate the gifts of wisdom these "fragile creators of chaos" bring to the family and the world. Each chapter unwraps a gift that Brennan received from one of the many teenage experiences of her seven children and invites the reader to reflect on how that gift might become a part of his or her life.

Calderone-Stewart, Lisa-Marie. *Know It! Pray It! Live It! A Family Guide to "The Catholic Youth Bible."* Winona, MN: Saint Mary's

Press, 2000. 800-533-8095, *www.smp.org*. This book leads you and your family on a tour through the Scriptures, where you will see what God's word has to say to life's most puzzling questions.

Chesto, Kathleen. *Exploring the New Family: Parents and Their Young Adults in Transition.* Winona, MN: Saint Mary's Press, 2001. 800-533-8095, *www.smp.org*. Introducing the idea of a new phase of life called postadolescence, the author takes a groundbreaking look at young adults, their families, and the influences that shape them.

Ford, Judy. *Wonderful Ways to Love a Teen . . . Even When It Seems Impossible.* York Beach, ME: Conari Press, 1996. 800-423-7087, *www.conari.com*. This is a handbook of tools to guide parents in the art of relating to their teenager. The author shows how to guide your teen toward a healthy adulthood while having fun in the process.

Kehrwald, Leif. *Parents and Schools in Partnership: A Message for Parents on Nurturing Faith in Teens.* Winona, MN: Saint Mary's Press, 2002. 800-533-8095, *www.smp.org*. This sixteen-page booklet offers practical ideas and suggestions for each family to be a community of faith (with its local parish) and to work with its Catholic high school as a faith community. Through family faith conversation, ritual and devotion, and outreach and service, schools and families can help young people learn about God, grow in relationship with God, and respond to the needs of others. Together schools and parents can form a powerful partnership to nurture a lasting and mature faith in teens.

McGrath, Tom. *Raising Faith-Filled Kids: Ordinary Opportunities to Nurture Spirituality at Home.* Chicago: Loyola Press, 2000. 800-621-1008, *www.loyolapress.com*. The author suggests how we can foster a healthy spirituality in our children while tending our own spirits as well. He shows how the hectic and ordinary moments of family life offer endless opportunities to live more deeply.

Pedersen, Mary Jo, et al. *More Than Meets the Eye: Finding God in the Creases and Folds of Family Life.* Winona, MN: Saint Mary's Press,

2000. 800-533-8095, *www.smp.org*. This book will awaken a family's awareness of God in all kinds of places and in common family experiences.

Pike, Maggie. *The Power of Discernment: Helping Your Teen Hear God's Voice Within.* Winona, MN: Saint Mary's Press, 2003. 800-533-8095, *www.smp.org.* This book shows that it really is possible to make such a lofty principle as discernment understandable, practical, and useful to a ten-year-old, a fifteen-year-old, and a young person on the brink of adulthood. Pike offers a method of spiritual discernment for dealing with such issues as peer pressure, friends, sexuality, change, family well-being, and others.

Rosengren, John. *Meeting Christ in Teens: Startling Moments of Grace.* Winona, MN: Saint Mary's Press, 2002. 800-533-8095, *www.smp.org.* In his eleven years teaching high school, Rosengren saw how "grace happens" when hanging out with teenagers. In this book he shares those encounters and empowers the reader to see God's gracious activity in the teenagers who are a part of his or her life.

Saso, Patt and Steve. *10 Best Gifts for Your Teen: Raising Teens with Love and Understanding.* Notre Dame, IN: Sorin Books, 1999. 800-282-1865, ext. 1, *www.sorinbooks.com.* The authors combine their expertise as a counselor and high school teacher with hard-knocks wisdom from the parenting trenches to offer practical and engaging guidance.

Stegman, Ronald. *Family Memories: Teenagers and Parents Share Their Stories.* Winona, MN: Saint Mary's Press, 1997. 800-533-8095, *www.smp.org.* This book serves as a resource for helping people share their own story about growing up and family life. The stories within make provocative and inspirational personal reading.

Vogt, Susan V. *Raising Kids Who Will Make a Difference: Helping Your Family Live with Integrity, Value, Simplicity, and Care for Others.* Chicago: Loyola Press, 2002. 800-621-1008, *www.loyolapress.com.* In her unique and thoughtful guide to raising socially conscious children, Vogt sets out to inspire, equip, and comfort parents in their awesome task of raising kids who will make a difference.

Acknowledgments

The scriptural quotations in this book are from the New American Bible with Revised New Testament and Revised Psalms. Copyright © 1991, 1986, and 1970 by the Confraternity of Christian Doctrine, Washington, D.C. Used with permission of the copyright owner. All rights reserved. No part of the New American Bible may be reproduced in any form without permission in writing from the copyright owner.

The words of Donna McIntosh, on pages 24–25, are from an interview conducted in the fall of 2002. Used with permission of Donna McIntosh.

The quotations by Pope John Paul II, on pages 26 and 99, are from his *Apostolic Exhortation to the Episcopate, to the Clergy, and to the Faithful of the Whole Catholic Church on the Role of the Christian Family in the Modern World (Familiaris Consortio),* part 3, "The Role of the Christian Family," at *www.vatican.va/holy_father/john_paul_ii/apost_exhortations/documents/hf_jpii_exh_19811122_familiaris-consortio_en.html.* Accessed May 5, 2003.

The quotation by the U.S. Catholic bishops on page 26, the extract by them, on pages 128–129, and the quotation by them on page 129 are from *Follow the Way of Love: A Pastoral Message of the U.S. Catholic Bishops to Families on the Occasion of the United Nations 1994 International Year of the Family* (United States Conference of Catholic Bishops [USCCB]), at *www.usccb.org/laity/follow.htm.* Accessed May 5, 2003.

The quotation by John Howard Payne, on page 27, is from his poem "Home, Sweet Home," in *Yale Book of American Verse,* edited by Thomas R. Loundsbury. Copyright © 1912.

The quotation by Angela Carter, on page 27, is from "My Father's House," in *Nothing Sacred: Selected Writings* (Gabriola Island, BC: New Society, 1976). Copyright © 1992 by Virago Press. Used with permission of Deborah Rogers Ltd., England and Time Warner Books UK.

The quotation by Robert Frost, on page 27, is from his poem "The Death of the Hired Man," in his book *North of Boston* (New York: Henry Holt and Company, 1915). Copyright © 1915 by Henry Holt and Company.

The paragraph describing the term *family career,* on page 31, is paraphrased from, and the excerpt about the four life processes, on page 36, the quotation about children needing a network of adults, on page 66, and the excerpt about the growing and changing family, on pages 74–75, are from *Family Ministry: A Comprehensive Guide,* by Diana R. Garland (Downers Grove, IL: InterVarsity Press, 1999), pages 115, 123, 560, and 113, respectively. Copyright © 1999 by Diana R. Garland. Used with permission of Intervarsity Press, P.O. Box 1400, Downers Grove, IL 60515. *www.ivpress.com.*

Kathleen Finley's definitions of the family life-cycle stages, on pages 32–33, and her excerpt about a life passage, on pages 34–35, are from an unpublished paper written by Kathleen Finley and commissioned by Saint Mary's Press in 1999.

The list of the four processes that unfold in families, on page 36, is adapted from "The Epigenesis of Relational Systems: A Model for Understanding Family Development," by Lyman Wynne and Kenneth Terkelson, in *Family Process,* volume 23, pages 297–318.

The quotation by Kenneth Terkelson, on page 36, is from "Toward a Theory of the Family Life Cycle," in *The Changing Family Life Cycle,* second edition, edited by Betty Carter and Monica Mc-Goldrick (Needham Heights, MA: Allyn and Bacon, 1989), pages 21–52. Copyright © 1989 by Allyn and Bacon.

The quotation about youth and parents, on page 45, the comments on Search Institute's 1992 survey of youth and parents, on page 48, the three items young people deem necessary for communication described on page 48, the quotation about the congregation's role in family relationships, on page 67, and the quotation about pastoral suggestions on page 68, are from *Passing On the Faith: A Radical New Model for Youth and Family Ministry,* by Merton P. Strommen, PhD, and Richard A. Hardel, DMin (Winona, MN: Saint Mary's Press, 2000), pages 48, 50, 51, 37, and 46, respectively. Copyright © 2000 by the Youth and Family Institute of Augsburg College. All rights reserved. Used with permission.

The statistics from Search Institute's 1992 survey of youth and parents, on pages 46–47, and the question regarding a young person's faith maturity, on page 103, are adapted from *Passing On the Faith* by Merton P. Strommen, PhD, and Richard A. Hardel, DMin, pages 48–50 and 145. Used with permission.

Craig Allan's survey questions and results, on pages 48 and 49, and his comments, on page 50, are from an interview conducted in the fall of 2002. Used with permission of Craig Allan.

The statistics from the U.S. Census Bureau, on page 55, are from a table titled "America's Families and Living Arrangements, March 2000," at *www.census.gov/population/socdemo/hh-fam/p20-537/2000/tabF1.txt.* Accessed May 7, 2003.

The statistics about children in single-parents households, on page 55, are from Unmarried America at *www.singlesrights.com/main.html.* Accessed May 7, 2003.

The statistics about women working outside the home, on page 56, are from the Family Education Network, at *www.familyeducation.com/article/print/0,1303,24-12688,00.html?obj_gra.* Accessed May 15, 2003.

The statistic about Nebraska families, on page 56, is from 2000 Census data at *www.usatoday.com/news/census/2002-05-21-childcare.htm.* Accessed May 7, 2003.

The statistics about women's first marriages, about women giving birth, and about women's educational attainment levels, on pages 56–57, are from the Family Education Network at *www.familyeducation.com/article/1,1120,24-12688-0-8,00.html.* Accessed May 7, 2003.

The words of Ann LaBeck, on pages 57 and 60, are from an interview conducted in the summer of 2002. Used with permission of Ann LaBeck.

The words of Shirlee Smith, on pages 57–58, are from her book *They're Your Kids, Not Your Friends* (Notre Dame, IN: Sorin Books, 2001), pages 13–15. Copyright © 2001 by Shirlee Smith.

The words of the three teenagers, on pages 61–62, are from *Almost Grown: Launching Your Child from High School to College,* by Patricia Pasick (New York: W. W. Norton and Company, 1998), pages 154–155, 78, and 149, respectively. Copyright © 1998 by Patricia Pasick.

The words of Maryelyn Scholz, on pages 65–66 and 67, are from an interview conducted in the fall of 2002. Used with permission of Maryelyn Scholz.

The statistic from the study sponsored by the Girl Scouts, on page 66, the excerpt about the support of the study, on page 66, and the excerpted paragraph and bullet points about how churches can build bridges, on pages 68–69, are from "What Teens Need from Adults," by Eugene C. Roehlkepartain, in *RespecTeen,* March 1992, newsletter, found in Search Institute's archives at *www. searchinstitute. org/archives/wtnfa.htm.* Accessed May 8, 2003. All rights reserved. Used with permission.

The excerpted bullet points on page 68 are summarized from "Mything the Point, Dealing with Denial, Getting the Facts," by Fred Kasischke and Audray Johnson, in *Adventist Review: Seventh Day Adventist,* August 11 and 18, 1993, as summarized in *Passing On the Faith* by Merton P. Strommen, PhD, and Richard A. Hardel DMin (Winona, MN: Saint Mary's Press, 2000), page 46. Used with permission.

The words of B. J. Levad, on pages 75–76, are from an interview conducted in the winter of 2003. Used with permission of B. J. Levad.

The excerpt on page 95 is from *Practicing Our Faith: A Way of Life for a Searching People,* edited by Dorothy C. Bass (San Francisco: Jossey-Bass Publishers, 1997), pages 8–9. Copyright © 1997 by Jossey-Bass Inc., Publishers.

The summary of family upbringing research, on pages 100–101, is from *The Search for Common Ground: What Unites and Divides Catholic Americans,* by James D. Davidson, Andrea S. Williams, Richard A. Lamanna, Jan Stenftnagel, Kathleen Maas Weigert, William J. Whalen, and Patricia Wittberg, SC (Huntington, IN: Our Sunday Visitor, 1997), pages 98–99. Copyright © 1997 by Our Sunday Visitor Publishing Division.

The quotation by John Roberto, on page 101, is from a source that is no longer in print. Used with permission of John Roberto.

The bulleted items summarizing study findings, on pages 109–110, are adapted from "Building Strong Families Fact Sheet: A Preliminary Study from YMCA/Search Institute on What Parents Need to Succeed," at *www.abundantassets.org/building.cfm.* Accessed May 12, 2003. Bracketed material was added. All rights reserved. Used with permission.

The story on pages 117–119 is from *Growing Up Girl: Sharing Your Heart with Your Mom,* by Eileen Pettycrew (Winona, MN: Saint Mary's Press, 2003), pages 81–83. Copyright © 2003 by Eileen Pettycrew. Used with permission of Eileen Pettycrew.

The bulleted items on page 123 are adapted from *The Dance of Anger: A Woman's Guide to Changing Patterns of Intimate Relationships,* by Harriet Lerner (New York: HarperCollins Publishers, 1997), page 183. Copyright © 1985 and 1997 by Harriet G. Lerner.

The quotation by Mitch Finley on page 124 is from a source that is out of print. Used with Mitch Finley's permission.

The quotation about the center of Jewish religious life, on page 127, is from "Family Orphaned by the Church," by Mitch Finley, in *National Catholic Reporter,* February 28, 1986, pages 11–12.

The quotation about Saint John Chrysostom, on pages 127–128, the quotation about Pope Leo XII's words regarding the family, on page 128, the quotation about the meaning of family spirituality, on page 129, and the excerpt about the relationship between the church of the home and the church of the parish, on page 130, are from *Building Christian Families,* by Mitch Finley and Kathy Finley (Allen, TX: ThomasMore, a division of Tabor Publishing, 1996), pages 14–15, 15, 18, and 16, respectively. Copyright © 1984 and 1996 by Mitch and Kathy Finley.

The quotation by Bernard Cooke, on page 128, is from his book *Sacraments and Sacramentality* (Mystic, CT: Twenty-Third Publications, 1983), page 92. Copyright © 1983 by Bernard Cooke.

The quotation by Pope Paul VI, on page 128, is from *Evangelii Nuntiandi,* his apostolic exhortation on evangelization, at *www.vatican.va.* Accessed May 14, 2003.

The quotations by Pope John Paul II, on pages 128, are from *Familiaris Consortio,* his apostolic exhortation on the role of the Christian family in the modern world, at *www.vatican.va.* Accessed May 14, 2003.

The excerpt on pages 132–133 is from *Experiencing God with Your Children,* by Kathy Coffey (New York: Crossroad Publishing, 1997), pages 13, 14, 16, and 24, respectively. Copyright © 1997 by Kathy Coffey Used with permission.

The words of Pope John Paul II, on pages 133–134, are from a homily he delivered in Perth, Australia, on November 30, 1986, as quoted from *A Family Perspective in Church and Society: A Manual for All Pastoral Leaders,* by the Ad Hoc Committee on Marriage and Family Life (Washington, DC: USCCB, 1988), page 21. Copyright © 1988 by the USCCB.

The words of Rev. Tom Boland, on page 134, are from his unpublished personal notes (Louisville, KY: Family Life Office, 1986), as quoted from *A Family Perspective in Church and Society* by the Ad Hoc Committee on Marriage and Family Life, page 22.

To view copyright terms and conditions for Internet materials cited here, log on to the home pages for the referenced Web sites.

During this book's preparation, all citations, facts, figures, names, addresses, telephone numbers, Internet URLs, and other pieces of information cited within were verified for accuracy. The author and Saint Mary's Press staff have made every attempt to reference current and valid sources, but we cannot guarantee the content of any source, and we are not responsible for any changes that may have occurred since our verification. If you find an error in, or have a question or concern about, any of the information or sources listed within, please contact Saint Mary's Press.